Chicago & Beyond

Chicago & Beyond
26 Bike Tours

Linda and Steve Nash

Follett Publishing Company/Chicago

"Sugar River Trail: New Glarus" was adapted from an article for *Country Gentleman* magazine. Copyright © 1979 The Country Gentleman Publishing Company. Used by permission.

Designed by Karen Yops.
Photographs by Linda Nash.

Library of Congress Cataloging in Publication Data

Nash, Steve, 1947–
    Chicago & beyond.

    1. Cycling—Illinois—Chicago region—Guide-books. 2. Bicycle touring—Illinois—Chicago region—Guide-books. 3. Chicago region, Ill.—Description and travel—Guide-books. I. Nash, Linda, 1954–   joint author. II. Title.
GV1045.5.I32C456   917.73   80-26895
ISBN 0-695-81561-X

First Printing

To Bert and Jeannette with love

Contents

Acknowledgments

Our thanks to the Forest Preserve District of Cook County and the Chicago Archicenter for information and guidance. Special thanks to the Mayor's Office of Special Events of the City of Chicago and the *Chicago Tribune* for permission to use routes, information, and several paragraphs from their excellent series of "Cycling Chicago" brochures.

Most of the chapter on the Sugar River Trail first appeared in our article in the Winter 1979 issue of *Country Gentleman* magazine and is used with the permission of the Country Gentleman Publishing Company.

Information for the Capron, Illinois, ride came from an excellent pamphlet compiled and produced by the Boone County Bicentennial Commission in cooperation with the Boone County Conservation District.

Introduction

Bicycle touring represents a happy solution to two common concerns these days: getting some exercise, preferably outdoors, and taking vacations that don't burn much gasoline.

Cycling is as good for the heart, lungs, and sense of well-being as many outdoor sports and better than most. It's the best kind of exercise, in which exertion isn't an end in itself but a by-product of pleasure. Except for the initial investment in a bike, cycling is cheap. Only minimal maintenance is required, and no special facilities are needed.

Chicago-area residents are especially lucky in the variety of rides available within a 100-mile radius of the city (the approximate range of this book). The terrain and the people change markedly from a bicycle path along Lake Michigan near downtown Chicago to the dairy farms of southern Wisconsin, and each route has its own appeal for those who glide silently through. There are no barriers of glass and sheet metal between you and the air and the sun; no traffic, parking, and gas refills to worry about.

Cycling can be as strenuous or as easygoing as you like. The rides in this book range from moderately difficult to easy, even for the inexperienced rider. We suggest that you begin with a ride of just a few miles or a bike path, which offers traffic-free cycling, and see how you feel when you're finished. Most people in average condition will be amazed to see how quickly their appetite grows and their stamina increases for the longer rides. Even the longest trip offers the option of turning back when you're tiring.

Some preliminary information begins each chapter in this book to help you decide which rides suit your mood and your schedule.

Location tells how far the ride is from Chicago "as the crow flies" and generally where it is on the map. **Distance** gives the length of the ride, excluding detours we suggest or those you may want to explore on your own.

The **Traffic** rating is important. If we could predict exactly how many cars and trucks you'd find on each ride, we'd deserve gold plaques in Bicycle Heaven. Unfortunately, traffic is an erratic phenomenon. We went to great lengths (literally) to find the least-traveled roads and watched carefully for the general traffic flow and any special problems before rating the rides.

If you're a camper, the **Camping** notes tell whether a ride includes parks with campsites. The **Difficulty** rating is based on a ride's length, its hills, and its traffic.

Riding time includes those factors too. It does not include time you'll almost certainly want to spend stopping at museums, wineries, parks, hikes, and the rest of the attractions you'll encounter. "Riding time" is a subjective rating, though our average pace matches that of most people we've ridden with. We're a little poky, if anything. You'll be able to place yourself in the low or high end of the range we give after your first few rides.

Directions tells you in fairly specific terms how to get from Chicago to the place where the ride begins. On a looped trip you can begin anywhere on the route, but *please note:* on any road, but country roads especially, the names and numerical designations change frequently and illogically. You may find, for instance, that an Illinois Avenue in town becomes Road 1118S at the city limits and Gunther Road in the next township or county. Often there are no road signs at all, so we've noted landmarks to tell you where to turn and in which direction to go.

Therefore, if you travel in the opposite direction from that indicated on the maps in this book, the roads' names and numbers may not apply—and you could easily get lost. So start anywhere, but heed the direction of the arrows on the map.

From time to time we mention a winery, a store, an interesting stop on the rides; we offer these as suggestions rather than recommendations in the strictest sense. In no case did we receive any gratuities from owners or employees in return for this.

Any bike in working order can handle these rides. The pleasure of cycle touring is enhanced, however, with the use of a ten-speed bike, whose light weight and gear range allow for much more flexibility and much less wasted energy.

Readers who have already tried cycle touring can anticipate many more good rides in these pages. But beginners are in luck too. You don't have to be experienced or an athletic aficionado to feel the breeze in your face or focus your eyes on the green Midwest horizon moving past. Just put your feet on the pedals and go.

Chicago & Beyond

Random Notes and Flat Tires

Clothing and coating

Cycling works up plenty of body heat even on a cool day, though much of it dissipates in the cyclist's self-made breeze. Plan on light clothing, especially shorts, during even mildly warm weather. Take sunglasses to keep out the glare, the bugs, and the wind, and remember to take some water along in a plastic bottle. The same sun that makes the corn and soybeans grow can make the cyclist wilt, and sometimes it's a long way to town.

Speaking of the sun, don't make the mistake of going all out for a tan and coming home parboiled and miserable. Always carry some suntan lotion along, unless it's definitely overcast and you can promise yourself it'll stay that way. And unless you're immune to mosquitoes or can't abide coating your skin with more goo, consider mosquito repellent. The lotion is cheaper but the aerosol is handier.

17

Doggie dos and don'ts

We met a farmer named Jim Fieldhouse and his wife as they were out cycling early one summer morning near their home in Culver, Indiana, and we asked what they did about dogs.

"I just don't pay any attention to 'em," said Mr. Fieldhouse. Ah, if only it worked that way for all of us.

You'll hear lots of advice about how to cope with dogs, all of it authoritative and much of it contradictory:

"You can ride faster than dogs can run—do it!" But what if you're a slow rider or going uphill? And anytime a dog gets in front of your wheels, you either have to stop fast or you'll crash.

"Let it know you're not scared and it will leave you alone." Not always true by any means, and anyway, what if you *are* scared, and with good reason?

"Get off your bike, lie flat on your back, and play dead." This passive resistance routine may work; we've never tried it. But it sounds risky.

"Hit the dog on the nose with your bicycle pump." Sure, but dogs are much quicker and more agile than a human straddling a ten-speed, flailing away with a pump. If you're moving while all this is going on, good luck trying to keep your balance.

We found this general advice and information from Jack Tuttle, a University of Illinois Extension small-animal veterinarian, to be helpful, partly because it isn't billed as foolproof.

"Be confident, but not competitive," Tuttle says. "If you speed up, the dog may be challenged. But if you go slow, he may be bored with you."

If you threaten the dog or try to outrun it, it may enjoy the challenge and continue the chase. Don't react angrily because the dog can sense an angry attitude.

Don't look the dog in the eyes because a stare-down is considered a test of superiority. If you stop your bike, keep perfectly still and don't make any sudden moves.

Rural dogs have more tendency to chase cyclists than city dogs, Tuttle adds. They will also have a larger domain they feel they need to protect, and it may include the road. Farm dogs are more confident than city dogs too.

You'll develop your own style with different dogs, as you do with people. When diplomacy fails though, we must turn from psychology to technology.

You'll find an aerosol antidog spray in many bike stores that is small enough to take on a ride, or you can mix ammonia and water in a squeeze bottle (use twice as much water as ammonia). But these only squirt a few feet, you can easily miss the dog, and a breeze can blow them back onto you, especially if you're riding.

We use what boat people call a "hailer." It's an excruciatingly loud horn powered, again, by an aerosol can. You might also try the pocket-sized antimugger "screechers" for sale in many places. Please don't point these things at your ears to test them.

A pocket-sized air horn of the kind described is available at some bike stores for about five dollars. But hold on a minute. The same manufacturer markets a larger but still handy version with a four-times-bigger aerosol that lasts much longer for nearly the same price. Look for it at boating stores.

Dogs are like potholes in the pavement—something a cyclist soon learns to watch out for without letting them spoil the trip. And unlike potholes, some dogs are even friendly.

Traffic and safety

Once in a while when you're idling along on your bike, try riding in a straight line as long as possible—the secret is to relax rather than tense up—and also practice looking over your shoulder without swerving too much to maintain your balance. Both these tricks help when you're coping with cars and don't have much room on the road. There's usually a route to the most interesting destinations and the most beautiful views that doesn't involve much traffic, but not always.

You're at a severe disadvantage to cars in both speed and "noticeability," and you must depend on your own good sense and awareness rather than that of the anonymous car or truck driver bearing down on you from behind. When the traffic is much too heavy and the road too narrow to be safe, get off and walk. It'll be a relief, and it won't last long—at least not on the rides we've charted in this book.

A rearview mirror with wide-angle vision makes it mostly unnecessary to glance over your shoulder or depend on your hearing to detect traffic coming from behind.

There are a few other things to look out for, and potholes and bumps head the list. Indiana and Illinois, proud and patriotic ornaments to the Republic though they may be, have really awful roads. That includes city streets and township roads we travel herein.

Another hazard is sand, dirt, and gravel. Your bike wheels are fairly securely connected to asphalt and concrete as you ride, but a small patch of sand is all that's needed to break the connection. Sand and gravel act like little ball bearings, especially if your front wheel is slanted in relation to the road or to your direction of travel. The faster you're moving and the more your wheel is leaning or turned, the greater the chance that you will skid. Anticipate! If you see sand, dirt, or gravel in your path, slow down, coast through, and don't turn or lean unless you're going very slowly.

The intersections of roads and railroad tracks are usually at right angles. If they are particularly bumpy, walk your bike over them, especially if you're not yet really confident on your bike. When they do not intersect at right angles, you must either walk or make sure you go straight across the tracks. The more you approach them at an angle, the more easily your front wheel will be forced out of your control by the tracks, and you'll take a spill.

If you are riding over any sort of bump or obstruction, do

what equestrians call "posting." Stand up slightly on your pedals while keeping a firm grip on your handlebars and lifting your behind off the bicycle seat. Let your legs be shock absorbers as the bike goes over the bumps. This is easier on your tailbone and on the relatively fragile rims of your wheels, both of which would have to take the shocks otherwise.

In the dark, always wear bright clothing. Use a good, strong light. Battery-powered models are preferable to generator sets because the latter don't work when you stop or go slowly. Make sure your bike has a full set of reflectors on back, front, pedals, and wheels. Go more slowly than usual because at high speeds your vision is much too limited to react to objects in the road.

Pedaling should be easy for you. If you're straining to make the pedals go around, always switch to a lower gear. As your strength builds, you'll go higher in the gear range. But don't strain.

If it's going to be hot, begin your trip as early in the morning as possible. It's the best time of day to see wildlife, avoid traffic, and beat the heat, and during any summer in the Midwest, it's the best time to ride.

Hey lady!

You're half of a bicycling couple—the female half—and your partner, whom you've envisioned riding slowly beside you, talking and looking at the scenery, is long gone up the road. He wants to push himself, to see what he can do. You are pushing yourself, and it's hurting.

This scenario occurs frequently enough that many couples who do much serious cycling have to deal with it. Women should understand that faster is not necessarily better. Steady, paced riding is easiest and most enjoyable. The important thing to keep in mind is that this is not competition. If you need to, go more slowly.

At a bike shop that carries seamless chamois shorts, special water bottles, and $800 frames, you may run into a purist who tries to talk you out of certain features that can make your ride easier. "Cheater" brakes, for instance, are levers that enable you to brake without leaning into the racing position. Although they may add an ounce or two of weight, they save a back that's not used to riding almost horizontally. Another item to consider is a seat shaped for women. It is wider where the pelvic bones meet the seat and provides more support for and less pressure on just one small area.

Accessories

As your interest in cycle touring grows, a multitude of accessories will tempt your eye. Some useful, inexpensive ones include toe clips, which harness the forward energy of your pedal stroke; a water bottle; a tire pump; a tool bag; a patch kit; a day pack or handlebar pack; and a rearview mirror. Much of the rest is a matter of taste rather than necessity for trips under 100 miles.

One of us likes to buy as many doodads and knickknacks as he can find to bolt onto his bike, including, at one time, a little propeller for the handlebars. The other one prefers to travel more lightly, keeping her accessories to a minimum.

There is a love of engineering among cyclists that can add to the enjoyment of the sport. For touring, though, it helps to be able to transcend the sprockets and cables and things, which you can enjoy at home in the garage if need be, and be open to the broader and quieter pleasures of the countryside you're traveling through.

One couple we know rode all over the East and Midwest, sometimes 100 miles in a day, on forty-pound (that's heavy for touring) bikes. They carried canvas saddlebags filled with pots, pans, canned food, cooking utensils, and tennis rackets. They didn't shave down their toothbrushes or buy freeze-dried food to save weight. But they did have a good time

and, until someone told them, didn't know they were sup-
posedly doing it "the hard way."

Bike maintenance

One way to remove those little mechanical concerns from
your mind is to make sure they're in good, reliable shape
before you begin your ride.

Some things to check before each outing:

Brakes—Check the brake shoes to make sure they're
aligned with the wheel rim; check the small nuts and bolts
which keep the calipers on the frame to see that they are
tight; check the brake cables. Are they rusty, frayed, or
worn? You'll be depending on them whenever you're on
your bike. Squeeze the brake levers and push on your bike.
The wheels should not move.

Handlebars—Check for play or wobble in the headset
(the bearings which let the handlebars turn in the frame)
and any sliding in the handlebars themselves.

Wheels—Check for wobble in the wheels and tighten the
quick-release levers or nuts if they are loose. They can vi-
brate loose or come uncocked during a long trip on a bike
rack too.

Tires—Check wear and hardness. Inflate to the pressure
indicated on the side of the tire.

Bike maintenance and repair is an adventure in itself. If
you don't have a greasy thumb, find a bike store with a
patient staff willing to answer your questions. If you like to
tinker, check out *Anybody's Bike Book* by Tom Cuthbertson
(Berkeley, Calif.: Ten Speed Press, 1979).

Your bike shop can recommend several tools, from rudi-
mentary to ritzy, to take along on your rides. We recommend, at the barest minimum, a tire-patch kit, three small
bike tire irons, a valve stem wrench, and a wrench, if
needed, to get the wheel off the bike. It's hard to be seri-
ously stranded in the Midwest—there's usually a farmhouse

nearby—but you can get past the flat-tire vexation on your own with a little patience.

Rule one: Don't try to ride on a flat tire or a soft one. It'll ruin the wheel fast.

If your tire has gone flat and you don't see nails, glass, or thorns in it, first check the valve stem in the center of the valve. Pump the tire up to put some pressure in it, remove the little cap on the valve, and put some saliva on the end of it. If bubbles appear, tighten the valve stem with the two tiny prongs on the end of the cap. If the cap has no prongs, use a valve stem wrench.

If you do find an offending object in your tire, leave it there. It may make it easier to find the hole in your tube later. Lay the bike on its side, derailleur up, and remove the wheel from the bike.

If the rear tire is the flat one, observe closely how the chain wraps around the rear sprockets and the derailleur. You'll have to duplicate that arrangement when you put the wheel back on.

Let the rest of the air out of the tire by depressing the center pin in the tire valve. Loosen the inside edge of the tire from all around the rim with your hands. See if you can work one edge of the tire over the edge of the rim by hand. Pull this side of the tire off the rim all the way around, but leave the other edge on the rim.

Now get hold of the tube with your fingers and carefully pull out and off the rim all but the part with the valve. You are now ready to find the hole and patch it.

But suppose you couldn't get the tire off the rim by hand. You'll need the small tire irons. Don't use a screwdriver or other replacement because it will poke holes in the tube and you'll be worse off than when you began. Even the tire irons must be used gingerly or the same thing will happen.

The iron has a notch in one end. Work the end without the notch under the edge of the tire, being careful not to get it under the tube too. If the tube gets pinched between the tire iron and the tire, you're likely to have another leak.

Pull back and down on the free end of the iron. Now's your chance to use that little notch. It hooks around a spoke to keep the iron in place while you're working on another section of the tire. Take the second iron (and a third, if necessary) and insert it under the tire (look out for the tube!) a couple of inches from the first, repeating the process. Now you're able to get one whole edge of the tire off the rim. Remove the tube carefully—all except the part with the valve on it.

You have the tube in your hands. Inflate it to slightly larger than normal size. Look for a leak and listen for a tiny hiss. If you think you've found it, use saliva or water to test it, watching for bubbles that get bigger. You can also dunk the whole tube and watch for bubbles.

If you've brought along a spare tube, which isn't a bad idea, you can skip all this, of course.

Follow the directions on the patch kit. Don't be impatient—this is the point you've worked hard to get to. Make sure the tube is clean before applying the patch, rough up the tube carefully with the little cheese grater that comes with the kit, don't get your fingers on the patch, and wait for the glue to dry.

Now for the hard part—getting the tire back on the rim. First check the inside of the tire for glass, rocks, thorns, and so on, then deflate the tube and work it back into the tire.

Work the tire and tube back onto the rim, section by section, until the last few inches on the opposite side of the wheel from the valve are all that remain.

Using your thumbs on the opposite side of the rim for leverage, try to pull that last section over the rim, being careful not to pinch the tube. You may be tempted to use the tire irons. Use your patience instead, if at all possible. At this stage the irons give good leverage but the tube is at risk, and you don't want to have to start all over.

Nice going, Ace. You're back on the road.

ILLINOIS

Rest stop behind the Wrigley Building, in the shadow of the riverfront skyline

Chicag-raphy
The Loop

Location:	Downtown Chicago, the Loop
Distance:	7 miles
Traffic:	Heavy isn't the word
Camping:	Unlikely
Difficulty:	Easy except for traffic
Riding time:	1½ hours
Directions:	Begin near Columbus and Roosevelt (12th Street)

Those brown and white signs saying Central Chicago Bike Trail you may have seen when you were in the Loop—if you're like us, your reaction was something like: "Who in his right mind would try riding a bike around here?"

It can be done, actually. Early Sunday mornings are best. Early Saturday (we're talking 5:30 A.M., at the time of year when there's enough light to see) is a second choice. Early on weekdays may be okay too, but after 6:30 you're risking a lot of walking or a lot of honking.

When you're pedaling down an empty Dearborn Street at
dawn, you'll have that funny feeling that this is some place
you're just not supposed to be, and that makes the ride all
the more enjoyable. All the cars and trucks and buses—or
most of them—have gone to the moon for the time being,
and you and your slender vehicle are the kings of the road.

Even this early there is some activity, some contrast between the undisturbed faces of those huge buildings—towering, smooth, uniform—and the beginnings of chaotic
interminglings down on the street. Indecipherable noises
ricocheting around these canyons: whooshes, squeals, as-
cending and descending notes in the scales of truck trans-
missions. A vagrant silhouetted in an alley. Two
warehousemen sharing a smoke in the doorway of a loading
dock.

Some other things to watch for:

Notice the sweet old water fountain at the beginning of
the trip, on the east side of Michigan Avenue, given long ago
to the people of Chicago by a grateful, or perhaps merely
admiring, Joseph Rosenberg of San Francisco. For reasons
unrecorded, on the fountain at least.

Alexander Calder's sculpture *Flamingo* is in Federal Center Plaza at Dearborn and Adams and sometimes enjoys the
company of more modest works of art. One recent compan-
ion comprised a dozen six-foot-long plastic tubes sticking up
out of a wooden frame. An air hose was attached to the
tubes and, in the early morning gloom, each tube was silently blowing soap bubbles up its length. Periodically a watery membrane would reach the top of a tube and pop, or
slop, depending.

"I don't know what it is either," a passing postal worker
told a pair of uncomprehending philistines at the time.

Near Dearborn and Monroe is Marc Chagall's *Four Sea-
sons* in the First National Bank Plaza. Pablo Picasso's fifty-
foot untitled sculpture, which he gave to the city in 1967, is
in Daley Plaza near Dearborn and Washington.

Madison Street used to be nicknamed "Bicycle Row" because of the many repair shops there during the bike craze
of the 1890s. In those pre-auto times when bikers' numbers
made them politically potent, they succeeded in having the
section of Jackson you'll ride between Michigan and Columbus blocked off under a "Yellow Ribbon Ordinance" that
temporarily banned trucks, wagons, and streetcars.

A good rest stop is a small plaza overlooking the Chicago
River just before the Michigan Avenue Bridge. Go through
the doors under the Wrigley Building Restaurant sign and
walk your bike down to the fountain. Here in the shade of
several buildings you can gaze at the flowerbeds and water
jet or look out over the river. The Wrigley Building was the
chewing-gum king's response to Mayor "Big Bill" Thomp-
son's invitation to business to move north in 1918.

The Michigan Avenue Bridge takes only a minute to open
and let boats pass through. Its foundations reach more than
100 feet below water level, and it is the only bridge of its
kind in the world.

On your right, just after you cross the bridge, is the site of
Fort Dearborn, the beginnings of Chicago. The fort was
built atop a small hill, which was later removed and used as
landfill.

Buckingham Fountain in Grant Park is 280 feet wide. It's
one of the largest and most beautiful fountains in the world.

Perhaps you'll want to park your bike and go shopping at
Lord & Taylor or Marshall Field's. Or go up to the top of
"Big John," the John Hancock Building. Or take a closer
look at the Water Tower, which Oscar Wilde called "that
castellated monstrosity with pepper boxes stuck all over it."
If so, here are the addresses of some facilities the city pro-
vides for parking and locking your bike: 11 West Wacker
Drive; 20 South Wacker Drive; 535 South State Street; 875
North Rush Street; 320 North LaSalle Street. You bring the
chain and the lock. Rates are fifty cents for twelve hours.

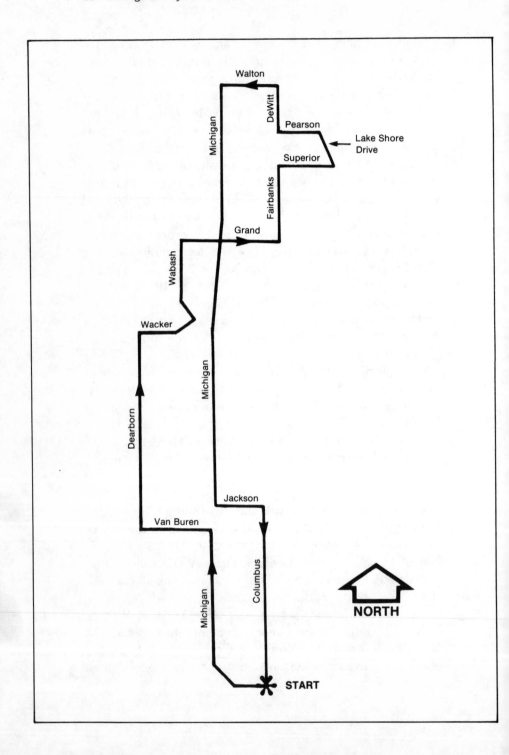

Chicag-raphy

Start at Columbus Drive, at the 11th Street pedestrian overpass, just west of the Grant Park bandshell off Michigan
Avenue. Go west over the overpass, then

(R) north on Michigan Avenue

(L) west on Van Buren

(R) north on Dearborn

(R) east on Wacker

(L) northwest on Wabash

(R) east on Grand

(L) north on Fairbanks. There is no sign, so look for the big,
      black Time-Life Building on the northwest corner. Then
      ride

(R) east on Superior

(L) north on Lake Shore Drive walk

(L) west on Pearson

(R) north on DeWitt

(L) west on Walton

(L) south on Michigan

(L) east on Jackson

(R) south on Columbus to Start.

Along Lake Michigan

Big-City Bikeway
The Lakefront

Location: Along Chicago's lakefront
Distance: 40 miles round trip
Traffic: No cars; heavy "people traffic" on the beach on weekends and holidays
Camping: None
Difficulty: Moderate because of length; easy if you ride in short stretches
Riding time: 6 hours
Directions: The trail begins at Bryn Mawr Avenue (5600 North) and heads south for 20 miles along the lake, parallel to Lake Shore Drive. You can start here or at the trail's southern terminus, below Jackson Park at the South Shore Country Club (at South Shore and 71st Street).

You haven't lived in Chicago long if you haven't heard about its lakefront bicycle path. We saw it described as "glorious" in a United States guidebook, and since we've lived in

35

the Midwest, we've heard it referred to by Chicagoans as everything from "fantastic" to "far out." Because the lake-front path is such an integral part of bicycling in Chicago, we felt our book would not be complete without it.

A couple of common-sense comments. If you like watching people as much as you do Lake Michigan and the city's skyline, you can cycle the path anytime. But if crowds bother you, don't pick a busy summer weekend or a holiday. Some branches of the path deposit you right on the beach, and although riding that close to the water is very scenic, the beach blankets and snack bars can create some frustration. You may find the crowds so thick in some spots that you can't really ride your bike, yet it's too unwieldy to walk it and it's out of the question to stop—the momentum of the crowd carries you along.

This is the kind of ride that can be taken many times over, each time with a sense of newness, of discovery. Besides the long list of attractions—museums, parks, the zoo, the conservatory—there are so many spontaneous things that can happen. We once passed a white-faced, pin-stripe-suited clown sitting formally atop a high-wheeler bicycle (also called a bone shaker). We stopped to listen to an antidraft rally, complete with several musical groups, and watched two teams play a fast-paced, somewhat makeshift, game of soccer.

It's fun to notice how the picnickers change as the ride changes neighborhoods. Since the path is almost all parks, you get quite a glimpse of cultures and habits by observing what there is to eat on the picnic blankets.

The exclusive apartments on the far north side are likely to have groups of singles sipping wine and nibbling cheese and crackers. Traveling south, the area near Lincoln Park reveals Chicago's diverse ethnic makeup. On a Fourth of July ride we passed large groups of, among others, Thais, Filipinos, Lebanese, Guatemalans, and Ecuadoreans. In this section we spied barbecued lamb, some spicy chicken, and even shrimp.

The people you see at the yacht club area just south of the Lake Point Tower apartment building (the one with the dark, curved glass) are usually not picnicking. They're getting ready to sail the lake. Any food they bring is enclosed in handwoven picnic baskets. After McCormick Place, the ambience changes again.

The more you ride the lakefront path, the more you'll notice the less obvious details. Try examining some of the miles of chalk graffiti on the concrete beach areas of the lakefront. The graffiti become a sort of crude mosaic stretching all the way to the lapping waters of the lake: two large heads smoking marijuana, butterflies with oversize wings, flags, skeletons, simple attempts at duplicating the beach scenery. New artists ruthlessly color over old masterpieces; misspelled swear words appear next to homespun philosophy and anonymous, loving initials.

It's not all chalk, either. Some of the sidewalk artists use spray paint to emblazon their messages, perhaps an attempt at permanence. "Visit Bongolia" stands out in sharp outline, as do "Frank Zappa" and "Summer Daze." Also look for a stone hippo and gargoyles on the bridge south of the Museum of Science and Industry.

We've compiled a noncomprehensive guide to give you a little background on sights you'll pass:

Heading south from the starting point, look for the Edgewater Apartments south of Bryn Mawr and north of Foster Avenue. The ornate, pink building is all that's left of the 1,000-room Edgewater Hotel. Built in 1916, it was host to big-band names like Tommy Dorsey and Glenn Miller. Most of the building was torn down, but senior citizens still live in the one remaining wing.

As you pass Foster Avenue, look for the back of the Saddle and Cycle Club. The club was built during the Gay Nineties when bicycling was a fad for the rich and stylish. The proper cycling outfit for a lady was a short skirt, a sailor

hat, low-heeled shoes, and thick leg coverings. A society ma-
tron rich enough to be part of the club probably had several
cycling parties on her calendar each summer.

At the foot of Montrose Avenue is the Montrose Harbor.
It's where rows of missiles aimed at Russia were set up during the cold war.

Next to the harbor is a bird sanctuary, home to 125 species of birds. If you take the ride early enough, you may
happen upon a morning "bird safari."

Around Lincoln Avenue you'll see Lincoln Park off to
your right. The dome is, of course, the Lincoln Park Conservatory, home to exotic flora like the fifty-foot fiddle-leaf rubber tree from Africa, a tapioca tree, and dozens of ferns.

Also in Lincoln Park is the Lincoln Park Zoo. Perhaps the
most interesting part of the zoo is the farm section, where
you can watch farm animals labor. The zoo also claims the
largest group of great apes in captivity.

At the foot of Ohio Street you'll pass the Chicago water
filtration plant, certainly not a scenic attraction. But we include it because of the sheer magnitude of its job. The plant
can process up to 1,700,000 gallons per day and usually pro-
cesses 960,000 gallons of water. It's the world's largest such
plant.

Past a string of yacht clubs and the downtown area you'll
see the Shedd Aquarium, another "world's largest," with 190
fish tanks and 7,500 specimens, including a coral reef where
fish are fed by divers several times daily.

Adler Planetarium has planetarium shows and exhibits
where you can learn about antique astronomy and modern
space devices.

The Field Museum of Natural History has that famous
exhibit of majestic African elephants and a new Anniversary
Hall, which explains how the museum came about.

Meigs Field, just south of the Shedd Aquarium, used to be

on an island. When the city hosted the 1933 World's Fair, they joined it to the mainland.

And finally, the Museum of Science and Industry, on the lakefront at 57th Street. Even if you've been there a dozen times you haven't seen all 2,000 displays.

Follow the path to its end at Lake Shore Drive and 71st Street.

These exuberant details have been called "architextures."
They abound in the Beverly-Morgan area.

Small-Town Chicago
Beverly Hills/Morgan Park

Location:	Beverly Hills/Morgan Park neighborhood in south Chicago
Distance:	Approximately 6 miles round trip
Traffic:	Moderate
Camping:	None
Difficulty:	Easy
Riding time:	2 hours
Directions:	Take Interstate 94 south to the 87th Street exit. Go west on 87th Street to Longwood. Turn left on Longwood and proceed south to 111th Street. Turn right and look for the Beverly Art Center on your left near the intersection with Bell. There is plenty of parking behind it.

A ride around Beverly Hills/Morgan Park is a ride up, down, and through a number of biggests and highests. The Ridge Historic District is the largest urban historic district in

America with some sixty historically and architecturally important buildings. It's on the highest land in Cook County, and the hilliest. And with thirty Prairie-style homes, some designed by Frank Lloyd Wright, it's one of the largest concentrations of this style of architecture outside of Oak Park.

The area, completely within the city limits of Chicago, is known for its friendliness and small-town aura. Aggressively promoted by the Beverly Area Planning Association as "the best of city and small-town living," the area has many multi-generation families who are committed to the neighborhood and to Chicago.

The Potawatomi Indians were the first residents of the area. Joseph Bailly, a French Canadian fur trader, visited here in 1822 because of the buffalo, bear, and wolves in the region. The first settlers came ten years later. DeWitt Lane built a log cabin in the area; his great-grandsons still live in the neighborhood.

The Vincennes Trail, used by traders and pioneers, passed through Beverly Hills/Morgan Park. A stagecoach line came here, and in 1852, the Rock Island Line began serving the town. Before 1900 wealthy business people and bankers came here to build their homes, many of which you'll see on this ride.

Beverly Hills, the portion of the ride north of 107th Street, was originally called Washington Heights. A resident from Beverly, Massachusetts, changed the name, partially because it means "beaver woods." Morgan Park, just to the south, was laid out by an early planner to resemble a park in his native England.

The area has almost every kind of architecture: the geometric, plain, but distinctive Prairie School houses; "gingerbread"-laden Victorians; Romanesque and Gothic churches; and ornate mansions. There are even some modern ranch-style homes and apartments. Many of the lots are large for the city and still preserve original woods. On the ride are some curving red-brick streets dating back to the turn of the century.

Geologically the area is also unique. Twelve thousand years ago it was an island in Lake Chicago, which was formed by water caught between a receding glacier and more elevated land. The island was made of sand and clay with bedrock underneath. The waves eroded part of the island, creating the first-gear Longwood Drive. As the lake retreated, the island became a ridge. Early settlers named it Blue Island because it appeared to be covered by a blue-tinged mist when seen from far away.

The neighborhood is rich in culture. The Beverly Art Center, where you begin your ride, includes a theater and was built with contributions from the community. There's an annual Architecture and Homes Tour that attracts 2,000 visitors, and an art fair each summer. Thirteen hundred people turned out for the area's first annual 10,000-meter run in 1978, and 1,000 came to the annual Snowflake Ball at the Evergreen Plaza (at one time another largest—this time in the world).

But don't let all these statistics distract you from the pleasant architecture and relaxed atmosphere of the area. It may not be the biggest and highest neighborhood anywhere, but it's got to be one of the nicest.

The following is a numbered reference guide that, along with the map, will help you spot some landmarks:

1. This is the community's showplace, Longwood Drive. Note the variety of architecture and you'll see why.

2. 10244 South Longwood Drive. The Irish Castle, built in 1886 at a cost of $80,000 and modeled after a castle called the River Dee in Ireland, is made of limestone hauled by oxcart all the way from Joliet. It was a girls' school and is now the home of the Beverly Unitarian Church.

3. 10036 Longwood Drive. Note the Spanish influence.

4. 9914 South Longwood Drive. This house was designed by Frank Lloyd Wright in 1908.

5. Look for the boulder and plaque commemorating the Vincennes Trail. The path was surveyed in 1834 and was popular with pioneers, Indians, and fur traders.

6. 9167 Pleasant Street. The Thomas Morgan Home was the home of the man Morgan Park was named after. Morgan farmed all the area you'll see in this ride, and the house before you is built partially on original granite boulders from Morgan's farm, called "Upwood."

7. 9326 Pleasant Street. Another Frank Lloyd Wright house, circa 1900.

8. You're now on the section of Longwood Drive created by glaciers.

9. 10821 South Drew. The Platt House is one of the oldest in Chicago and the oldest in this area. It was constructed in 1870 by Platt, an English immigrant, for his wife, a former lady-in-waiting of Queen Victoria's. There's an 800-year-old oak in the yard, and the house hides a secret room once used to conceal runaway slaves as part of the Underground Railroad.

10. These Prospect Avenue homes were occupied by some of the neighborhood's most prominent citizens. For example, the Blackwelder House at 10910 South Prospect was owned by the area's first woman voter, the house at 10924 belonged to Morgan Park's first physician, and at 10934 lived Henry Crosman, founder of the Chicago Opera Company in 1872.

11. The Rock Island Railroad station was built in 1892 to connect the "suburban" Beverly/Morgan area with urban Chicago.

12. 11071 South Hoyne. This library was built by one of the town's original developers.

13. 2153 West 111th Street. The Beverly Art Center, located on the campus of the Morgan Park Academy, has a 460-seat theater and displays most of the John H. Vanderpoel Collection of twentieth-century art.

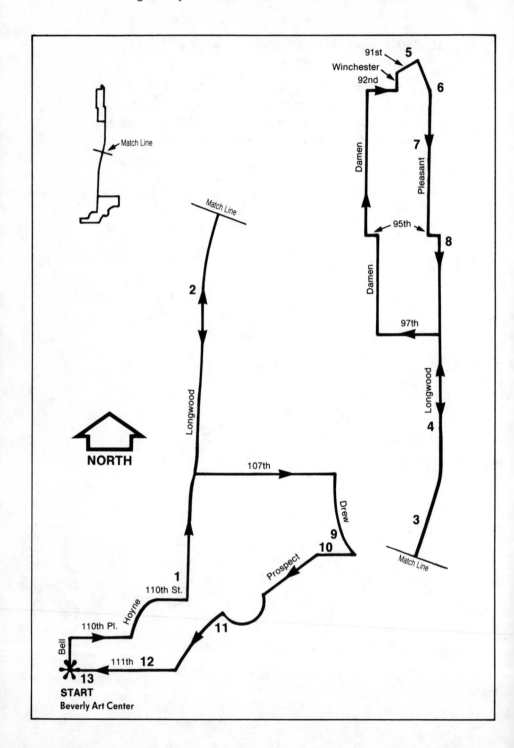

Small-Town Chicago

Begin at 111th Street and Bell at the Beverly Art Center. There's plenty of parking behind the art center. Go north on Bell, then

(R) east on 110th Place

(L) north on Hoyne

(R) east on 110th Street

(L) north on Longwood Drive

(L) west on 97th Street. Go two blocks, then

(R) north on an unmarked street that you'll learn is Damen Avenue

(R) east on 92nd Street

(L) north on Winchester

(R) northeast on 91st Street. The Dan Ryan Forest Preserve is down this street. You can picnic there. Retrace path to

(R) south on Pleasant Street

(L) east on 95th Street, one-half block

(R) south on Longwood Drive

(L) east on 107th Street

(R) south on Drew Street

(R) west on Prospect Avenue and take the original brick street around Prospect Park near the railroad crossing

(R) west on 111th Street and a tough short hill. Continue up 111th to the Beverly Art Center.

Pullman's Legacy
South Pullman

Location:	South Pullman in Chicago
Distance:	Approximately 2 miles
Traffic:	Light
Camping:	None
Difficulty:	Easy
Riding time:	1 hour
Directions:	From Highway 41 (South Shore Drive) take 95th Street east to Cottage Grove. Turn left on Cottage Grove to 111th Street and the circle of historical markers in front of the Florence Hotel.

The time: 1893
The place: The Pullman Community. Back then it was world famous as a model city offering the factory worker everything in comfort and convenience—reasonable rents on homes with flush toilets, hot and cold running water, and

central gas lighting; an 8,000-volume public library; a fifty-shop arcade; and an ornate theater offering the likes of *Tuxedo* and *Uncle Tom's Cabin*. What more could a railroad-car-company factory worker want?

A lot more. Just one year later this model community turned into a model of labor unrest when twelve workers were killed during a violent strike. The strikers were joined by the American Railway Union, which boycotted all Pullman luxury cars throughout the country and helped crush the community's already dented image.

It's hard to pinpoint exactly what went wrong, but many attribute the community's demise to the factor responsible for its creation: the personality of George M. Pullman. You'll get a feel for the force behind the rows and rows of uniform brick residences and the imposing public buildings when you cycle around the South Pullman district.

The ride is very short, but it's the kind of spin where there's so much to see that your bicycle glides slowly along while you look in every direction. You won't feel exercised; we had no idea we'd traveled even two miles when we happened upon our car. But if you do this in conjunction with the nearby Beverly Hills/Morgan Park ride, you've gone a respectable distance for a day.

It's impossible to understand the community without knowing a little about Mr. Pullman. A driving, ambitious, creative man, he conceived of a city that would radically increase worker productivity because of superior living conditions. He tried to think of everything. Sewage from the community was pumped three miles south to fertilize a model farm that produced vegetables and dairy products consumed in Pullman. The town was built on the shores of Lake Calumet, and clay from the lake bottom made the brick houses you see today. Many homes had skylights upstairs, and the town had landscape crews, a nursery, and a greenhouse to keep it looking pretty. There was even an artificial lake with a giant water jet in the middle of it.

But Pullman was ignorant of human psychology. In executing his dream, he tried to impose his standards on everyone, and they were quite rigid. An extremely clean man, Pullman kept his community spotless. Garbage was collected daily and fresh cans set in place of the full ones. Produce and meat could be sold at only one place in town, he decreed, because of sanitation.

And Pullman had strong morals. He objected to workers' drinking and allowed only one saloon in the community. But the town did adjoin the rest of the world, and another entrepreneur, Joseph Schlitz, built two blocks of saloons and stables just across the tracks from Pullman to accommodate the overflow crowd. Pullman believed churches should pay rent and charged them just what he would "any other business," $3,600 per year. For several years there was only one church in Pullman.

He believed in rank and hierarchy, as you'll see when you examine the homes in the district. The unskilled workers who had just arrived lived in some of the multi-family dwellings on Langley. They shared bathrooms. Skilled laborers lived in apartments and plain single-family homes. As your status increased, so did the moldings and doors on your home and the height of your ceiling.

The workers' strike and the depression of 1894 heralded the end of the experimental community. When Pullman died in 1897, the houses were sold to residents.

Many fourth-generation Pullmanites still reside in this sixteen-square-block area, surrounded by what urban planners delicately refer to as "deteriorated" neighborhoods. If it hadn't been for these longtime residents, the community might have been razed in 1960 to make way for industry.

But it has been saved, and it's now a National Historic Landmark with big plans for the future. The Historic Pullman Foundation now conducts walking tours of the area the first Sunday of every month, and there are other events planned. We happened upon a neighborhood festival with hula hoop contests for the kids and free jazz for their parents. The foundation wants to restore the Arcade building to a specialty shopping center and start a museum of Pullman railway history nearby. They've already begun restoration of the lovely Florence Hotel, named after Pullman's favorite daughter. Lunches and Sunday brunches are served at the hotel as well as at the Pullman Club nearby, in another historic building.

Here's a number-coded guide to some of the area's buildings. Inquire at the hotel for more information on any of them.

1. The Florence Hotel once entertained such luminaries as Jay Gould, Diamond Jim Brady, and Lillian Russell. Built to house foreign dignitaries during the Columbian Exposition in Chicago, and later populated by vagrants and fleas, it is almost completely restored. Look for the twelve-foot mirror in the ladies' sitting parlor downstairs, the solid cherry woodwork, and the mahogany four-poster bed in Pullman's suite. Ask clerks of the hotel to show you the last piece, which is adorned with carved pineapples.

2. The Pullman Palace Car Company's administration building is at the corner of East 111th Street and Cottage Grove Avenue. The luxury cars were built assembly-line fashion in this structure, which was originally 700 feet in length.

3. 111th Street used to be Florence Boulevard. It divided the industrial buildings from the homes. The factories faced Lake Vista, the three-acre artificial lake above which the company would set off fireworks to entertain residents.

4. The Pullman Club used to be an executive gathering place.

5. On 111th Street, between St. Lawrence and Langley, are the eight- and nine-room homes built for Pullman executives.

6. The buildings on the left side of Langley housed low-paid migrant workers.

7. Market Hall, surrounded by a circular street, was built to counteract the monotonous grid structure of the rest of the community. Vendors rented space to sell meat and vegetables. One vendor was the father of "untouch-able" Eliot Ness.

8. On Champlain you'll find five-room row houses and two-flat and four-flat houses.

9. On this section of Langley you'll see the three-flat build-ings where middle-class workers lived. They paid about twelve dollars rent per month.

10. On the southwest corner of St. Lawrence and 113th Street is the Pullman Elementary School.

11. The Cottage Hospital, at 11217 St. Lawrence, was the company hospital.

12. At the corner of 112th and St. Lawrence is the Green-stone Church, probably so named because the New England serpentine stone looks almost emerald after a rain. The only church Pullman allowed in the commu-nity, it stood vacant for three years because of the $3,600 rent Pullman charged. His objective was to make a 6-percent profit on the building.

13. The building across the street from the church, on the southwest corner of 112th and St. Lawrence, is the for-mer home of Pullman's official timekeeper, John Hop-kins. An adamant Democrat who quarreled with the

firmly Republican Pullman, Hopkins moved his business out of the Pullman Arcade and later became mayor of Chicago.

14. On the northeast corner of 112th and St. Lawrence is the Greystone Mansion, built for Dr. Faye, one of the town's doctors.

15. Facing the hotel on 112th Street are the homes of foremen and company officials.

16. This Citgo gas station used to be the Pullman stables. Look for the wooden horses' heads with the sign Pullman Motor Stables over the garage door. Because of their "unsanitary habits," horses and other animals were not allowed in the community.

17. Where the American Legion Hall stands was the Arcade, which was a forerunner of modern shopping malls. Completely enclosed, it included fifty shops, a theater, a post office, and a library. It had two multi-story walkways and was the largest commercial shopping structure in the Chicago area.

18. Pleasant Park used to be called Arcade Park. It was restored in 1977.

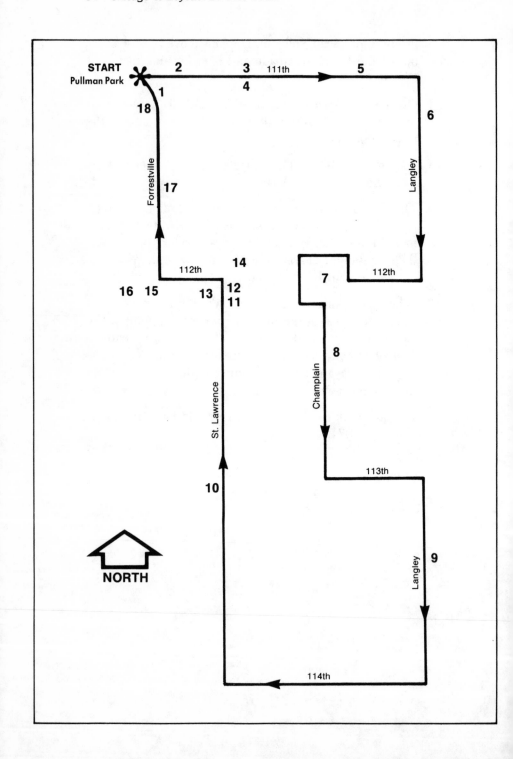

Pullman's Legacy

Start at the Pullman Park circle of historical markers at Cottage Grove and East 111th Street. Then go

(R) east on 111th
(R) south on Langley
(R) west on 112th and circle around Market Hall
(R) south on Champlain
(L) east on 113th
(R) south on Langley
(R) west on 114th
(R) north on St. Lawrence
(L) west on 112th
(R) north on Forrestville to Pullman Park.

Obliging giraffe illustrates practicality of long necks at the Brookfield Zoo

Backyard Wilderness
Cook County

Salt Creek Trail

Location:	Western Cook County, about 15 miles from Chicago
Distance:	12 miles round trip
Traffic:	Nonexistent on separate bike path; heavy on short stretch near Brookfield Zoo
Camping:	None nearby
Difficulty:	Easy
Riding time:	2 hours
Directions:	Take the U.S. 34 exit (Ogden Avenue) from Interstate 294. Go east on 34 to Bemis Woods entrance on your left. In the preserve, drive past the first parking area until you see the sign for the bike trail.

Salt Creek is an obviously urban bike trail. Often you'll share the path with groups of skaters rolling powerfully along in a stampede of wheels, old men pedaling slowly on rusty three-speeds, women joggers with large dogs for protection, and groups of teenagers sitting by the trail just checking out all the rest of the people. Although you can't exactly zoom through this trail, the slower pace can be enjoyable, especially if you like to people-watch.

The slower pace is probably the best thing anyway, considering the layout of the trail. There are many intersections, and some come upon you without warning. To find yourself right on the edge of a four-lane, bumper-to-bumper-traffic highway is a breathtaking experience, especially if you're going top speed. Although heavily used, this trail is very rough in spots. We saw one bicyclist lying on the trail with an injured knee, his bent bicycle at his side. The path had taken a plunge underneath some railroad tracks. Where the trail darkened the concrete ran out, and some rough boards and rutted earth took over. Taking this at any more than a slow coast almost guarantees a fall.

The sign at the forest preserve says the trail leads to Brookfield Zoo. That it does—almost. The trail stops about one-quarter mile from the zoo, requiring you to ride, or better yet, walk your bike, along a razor-thin dirt path next to a very busy street.

But if you like watching the animals, your destination will be worthwhile. Walk your bike down to the parking lot and entrance to the zoo. You can lock it there at special bike racks within view of the parking attendant. Another plus: you don't have to pay the $1.50 parking fee.

After seeing an assortment of characters on the Salt Creek trail, the mammals at the Brookfield Zoo may not look that strange. But even the most skeptical visitor can probably find something a little unusual to peer at, like an okapi, a zebra-striped giraffelike animal from Africa, or a nocturnal kiwi bird that can't fly and roots for earthworms all evening.

The predator ecology exhibit features the nocturnal environments of five small predators. You can stroll through the

Sahara Desert, the Rocky Mountains, a Himalayan pass, and a tropical forest and view animals like lynxes, margays, and sand cats.

The zoo's 200 acres and twenty-four major exhibits can be overwhelming. Why not return several times? If you take early-morning or late-evening bicycle trips, you're likely to see the most interesting animal activities—many creatures who rest or sleep all day are stirring at this time.

North Branch Trail

Location:	The north end of Chicago and the suburbs of Skokie, Niles, Morton Grove, and Glenview
Distance:	20 miles round trip
Traffic:	Nonexistent; trail crosses a few busy intersections
Camping:	None
Difficulty:	Easy
Riding time:	2½–3 hours
Directions:	Take the Edens Expressway (I-94) to the Caldwell Avenue exit. Follow the signs for Caldwell Woods.

The best thing about the North Branch bicycle trail, in our opinion, is that you can really bicycle on it. Removed from the hazards of city traffic and the distractions of pot-holed roads, this mostly smooth, wide path with the miles and even the turns marked out for you eliminates all distractions. It's a good kind of trail for coasting along and looking at the trees or for whizzing by in a sweaty streak, stopwatch in hand, trying to beat an earlier record.

You'll hear people—picnickers, baseball players, maybe even voices over the loudspeaker from a church carnival or a flea market—but the trail insulates you from their comings and goings. You share the path mostly with other cyclists and joggers, and if you take the markers' advice and keep to your own lane, you'll have a safe trip down this bicycle highway that allows you to be as speedy or as relaxed as you like. You won't even have to slow for joggers on part of it. They have a separate trail parallel to yours.

The region is rich in history. Several Indian trails crisscross the terrain and Indian campfires burned where we now see lush meadows. In one way, the Indians were responsible for the creation of some of this forest preserve. A man named Billy Caldwell, of both Indian and European ancestry and a friendly intermediary with the Ottawa, Potawatomi, and Chippewa of the region, helped convince the Indians to move from the Chicago area to west of the Mississippi, allowing their lands to be settled by pioneers. As a token of the government's appreciation, Caldwell received the 1,600 acres now named Caldwell Woods.

Also in the preserve is what looks like merely an overgrown clearing, bursting with wildflowers, tall grasses, and thick, swaying weeds. This, a sign proclaims, is a small portion of what much of the Midwest once looked like—a slice of original prairie preserved for urban and rural eyes.

A couple of complaints about the trail: garbage filled many of the cans and overflowed onto the grass in some spots, and the smell from the "sanitary" facilities can be literally unbalancing!

Frank Lloyd Ride
Oak Park

Location: Oak Park, a suburb of Chicago
Distance: 2½ miles
Traffic: Occasionally heavy, especially on major
                arteries
Camping: None
Difficulty: Easy, but be very careful in traffic
Riding time: 1½–3 hours
Directions: Take the Austin exit off Interstate 90
                north to a left turn on Lake Street.
                Begin at Unity Temple, at the corner of
                Lake and Kenilworth.

If you don't care anything about architecture and you're sure you never will, you need this ride like the Titanic needed ice.

Now if you don't *know* anything about architecture, that's different, because that's what this ride is for. It takes you past different styles of residential architecture just as we were taken by a volunteer guide from Chicago's Archicenter ("a nonprofit organization working to help people develop a greater awareness of our built environment"). We offer you here what we hope is a helpful blend of his comments and our own about houses you'll see.

This ride is one of several tours in the Chicago area that the Archicenter sponsors. Phone their offices for a current schedule. When we started, we didn't know a Queen Anne from a Quonset hut, but we enjoyed learning.

If you do the ride on a Sunday morning, you can take a lecture tour of the Unity Temple and the nearby neighborhood for three dollars. Half the money goes to the Archicenter, half to a temple restoration fund.

The temple's architect was Frank Lloyd Wright, a name you'll be seeing a lot of from here on. It's hard not to appreciate his fiercely independent ideas after seeing them materialized in wood, glass, and stucco along the streets of Oak Park and River Forest and comparing them with the designs of his contemporaries.

Wright lived in Oak Park for twenty years until 1909. Ernest Hemingway was born here as was Edgar Rice Burroughs, town boosters will tell you. Before 1902 Oak Park was considered part of Cicero; it was only a small settlement with big, open tracts of prairie around it.

The temple was built to replace another Unitarian church, which burned down in 1905. Wright's intent was to incorporate Unitarian ideas of simplicity and openness in the design and to achieve "nobility" within his budget of only $45,000. (He didn't succeed in staying within his budget.) The design also reflects the influence of an extended visit Wright made to Japan.

Take a look at the churches across the street from the temple, all modeled after the patterns of European cathedrals of hundreds of years before, and all standing when Wright began work. Imagine the consternation of the devout of Oak Park as Wright's concrete began to take form. It was like nothing else they had ever seen, and it was an affront to most of them. He had even put a blank wall on the main street and hidden the entrance on Kenilworth because he disliked the dust and noise and streetcars.

As you ride down Kenilworth, you'll see three houses that Wright wouldn't have liked on the northwest corner at the intersection with Erie. Imitations of Victorian styles and the shell design on the lintel over one porch (a borrowed Venetian device) didn't "belong" in the Midwest, bursting with development and new ideas, according to Wright.

Here's a numbered guide and some background information about the architectural landmarks along the trail:

1. At 334 Kenilworth is the H. P. Young House, combining the Tudor style with some of Wright's fresh ideas. It is by no means the departure that the temple was. Wright designed the Young House when he was twenty-eight, the period when he was said to be "struggling to find himself."

2. On the northeast corner of Forest and Chicago is Wright's home and studio, now a museum, where you can also take a tour (call for times) and hear more about his ideas, personality, and influence.

3. At 1019, 1027, and 1031 Chicago, you'll see three Wright houses that show even less originality, especially the one with the big round turret that looks like a silo with a dunce cap. This is a common feature of the Queen Anne style. The three houses are known as Wright's "bootleg" or "bread and butter" houses. He built them on the sly, while under contract to another architect and not allowed to make such side deals, in order to make more money.

4. The next stop comes after a long swoop into River Forest that takes you to 515 Auvergne Road, the William Winslow House, built in 1893. A group of Japanese architects on a recent tour were said to have gone "com-

pletely berserk" with appreciation on seeing it, and it is one of the most memorable structures on this tour. When built, it was completely alone on a vacant landscape, making it an even more dominant feature.

It was Wright's first commission as an independent architect, so it is another transitional design, but it has several features that foretell the Prairie School of residential architecture he later inaugurated: it has a "hipped" roof, which rises at a flat angle to a central chimney; horizontal lines dominate (compare with Queen Anne styles); and the roof overhangs are broad, helping make the house seem lower and flatter.

The arched structure on the side is a "porte cochere," where carriage passengers could disembark in inclement weather.

5. Wright was still experimenting in 1895 when he designed 530 Edgewood Place, a house built for Chauncey Williams. The roof seems to make this two-story house appear single-story because it is so broad and flat. The arch at the door, with a beaded design, stems from Wright's apprenticeship under architect Louis Sullivan.

On this block, look for an Italianate brick farmhouse with a characteristic flat arch over windows and doors in the shape of a dignified and doleful eyebrow. The house has black shutters and ornamental "gingerbread" wood decorations and is immaculately kept.

6. William Drummond, who worked in Wright's studio and was obviously a devotee of the Prairie School, built the house at 559 Edgewood in 1911. He introduced elements of English designs at 555 Edgewood to satisfy his clients and also built at 560 Edgewood.

7. 603 Edgewood Place was built for Isabel "Izzy" Roberts, Wright's private secretary, in 1908. A tree grows through its dining room. There is an arresting diamond

pattern in the leaded-glass windows, which are original. The house was stucco but was rebuilt in brick in 1955. The living room is two-story. This is the first pure Prairie School house so far on the ride. Note its "ground-hugging horizontality"; another characteristic feature is that the house is cross-shaped or "cruciform," as is the Unity Temple.

Wright's residential designs are said to have "destroyed the box," the boxy shapes that dominated other styles, such as the hand-me-down European derivatives. He meant the design to be not only bold and clean-lined but also functional and more livable inside.

This was a time when the use of servants was declining among the wealthy, and with it the need for privacy and separation between rooms. Rooms in Wright's houses flow into one another and have many fewer doors and partitions.

The exteriors, though, are much more quiet and private than those of typical houses of the time, with side rather than front entrances that don't break up the symmetry and the horizontal lines of the front of the house.

8. At 562 Keystone is the house Wright built for a man named Ingalls in 1909, another cruciform, with urns out front (you've seen them before too) and a somewhat hidden "front door." This is said to be a typical Prairie School house. The windows here are striking, and the green-on-green paint accents are quiet and harmonious. Our guide recalled the saying that "architecture is frozen music." The music in some other houses here is reduced to honks and wheezes by comparison with Wright's—they have not aged as well.

9. At the end of the block is a huge white imitation of a French Empire style with a mansard roof (pitched steeply and flat on top). American appropriation of European styles was our way of exhibiting wealth, status,

connections. Sometimes a number of centuries and countries are mixed together oddly in a single home.

10. Keystone is quite a street. On the east side are replicas of Norman and English houses and, on the opposite side, a Federal Revival design.

11. The Arthur Davenport house at 559 Ashland was one of the first Prairie houses, built in 1901. It is very Japanese. Note the drain spouts blending into the lines of the protruding eaves. The roof is of a type called "warped gable."

12. At 628 Bonnie Brae is a house built by a Wright disciple, Charles Purcell, in 1909. The porch is integrated into the house rather than just "stuck on," as are others on this block. The garage, visible in the rear, is said to be "a triumph."

13. The Heurtley House, 318 Forest, 1902. Wright again. Terrific.

There are several more Wright houses on the remainder of this ride. See if you can spot them.

River Forest museum piece

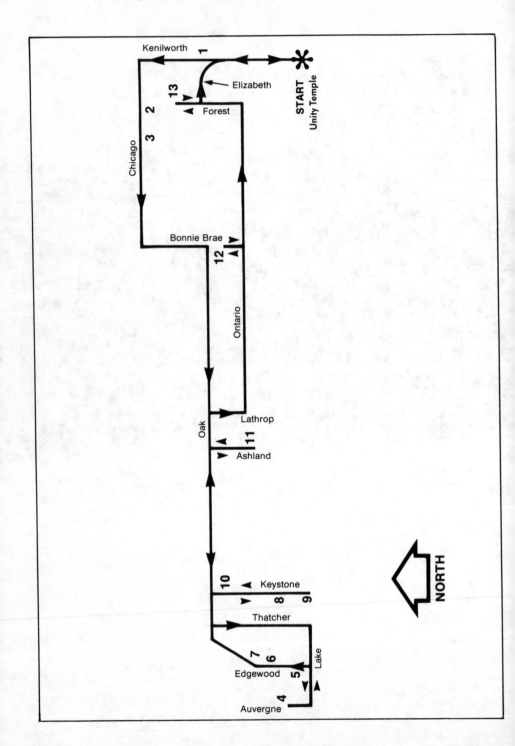

Frank Lloyd Ride

Begin at Unity Temple at the corner of Lake and Kenilworth in Oak Park. Go north on Kenilworth, then

(L) west on Chicago
(L) south on Bonnie Brae
(R) west on Oak into River Forest
(L) south on Thatcher
(R) west on Lake
(R) north on Auvergne. Retrace path back to Lake. Then
(L) east on Lake for one block
(L) north and east on Edgewood
(R) east on Oak
(R) south a block on Keystone, then return to Oak and go
(R) east on Oak
(R) south on Ashland a half block. Return to Oak, then
(R) east on Oak
(R) south on Lathrop
(L) east on Ontario
(L) north on Bonnie Brae to the house at 628. Return to Ontario and go
(L) east on Ontario
(L) north on Forest to the house at 318. Return south to
(L) east on Elizabeth, a cul-de-sac. Hop the curb and go
(R) south on Kenilworth to Unity Temple.

The Midwest's New England
Innermost Evanston

Location:	Just a mile or two north of Chicago in Evanston
Distance:	5½ miles
Traffic:	Light on separate bike path; moderate to heavy on some city streets
Camping:	None
Difficulty:	Easy
Riding time:	1–2 hours
Directions:	From downtown Chicago, take Lake Shore Drive north along the lake. It becomes Sheridan Road. Follow it over the Evanston city limits. Look for Clark Square Park on your right. If you reach the Baha'i Temple, you know you've gone too far.

There's a secret side of Evanston. It's not the side you see when you've missed the far north side of Chicago and instead found yourself whizzing along the tree-lined streets of

Evanston's Sheridan Road, with too much traffic to let you turn around. And it's not even the little ethnic restaurant that your neighbor recommended off Chicago Avenue or that funny ice-cream parlor you read about in *Chicago* magazine. It's the Evanston you see when you slow down the pace and really look, for the city's graceful, gentle sights take time to appreciate.

You might have seen this Evanston as a child and marveled at big, fancy houses that looked 100 times taller than you were. But it's even more special today when you take it by bike.

The largely residential city on the shores of Lake Michigan has 75,000 residents. It's a college town in the strictest sense; there are five institutions of higher learning within the city limits. And Evanston is headquarters to a wide range of staid institutions such as Rotary International, the Methodist Church, and the Women's Christian Temperance Union. The imposing churches, the arbored streets, the Gothic mansions next to Prairie-style split-levels—all exhibit a sense of permanence, of seclusion. The streets are dotted with bicyclists, and the parks are full of bearded dads and blue-jeaned moms swinging and playing with their children.

You're not in a big city but definitely not in a small town either. In fact, the town was so special it became known as the "finest New England village in the Middle West." That ambience is still here, and it makes for a blissful ride.

Marquette landed at Evanston in 1674, but the town was not officially settled until almost 200 years later. Perhaps its most important event was the opening of Northwestern University in 1855. The city is named after John Evans, one of the university's founders.

Part of the ride winds through the university's ivy-covered lakeshore buildings and past the Dearborn Observatory. Northwestern has 10,000 students and offers guided walking tours of the stately campus every weekday at 2:00 P.M. and Saturdays at 12:00 noon. They begin at 633 Clark Street.

Evanston has laid a separate bicycle path right alongside the lake and another one along a drainage channel through a series of parks and an arboretum. Other streets have marked bike lanes, and still others, like busy Sheridan Road, have signs insisting that bikers use the sidewalk! Your route passes by and near some inviting eateries and expensive but intriguing shops.

The lakefront bike path ends just short of the Grosse Point Lighthouse, built after a shipwreck on Lake Michigan took 300 lives. The Evanston Art Center, with exhibits by local artists, is also here, along with a sizable beach.

One detour off this path leads to a modest home at 1730 Chicago Avenue. It takes a closer look at the worn plaque on the door to discover that this is where the Women's Christian Temperance Union started. The organizer of the worldwide political coalition, Frances Willard, lived here in this 1865 home with her family, and her group still runs the organization from a building in the back. You can tour this National Historic Landmark Monday through Saturday from 8:30 A.M. to 5:00 P.M.

A second trail detour leads to the home of another prominent former resident. Charles Dawes, vice-president under Calvin Coolidge, gave his ornate mansion to Northwestern hoping it would become the home of the Evanston Historical Society, which it did. Open from 1:00 to 5:00 P.M. every day except Wednesday and Sunday, it has several rooms from the 1910–1920 period, displays of costumes, antique toys and dolls, Indian artifacts, and other items of interest.

It's a nostalgic trip in this New England village hundreds of miles from Cape Cod, and there are plenty of parks through the ride where you can dismount, lean against a spreading tree, and contemplate your way into the past.

The Midwest's New England

Begin at Clark Square Park at Sheridan Road and Kedzie Street in Evanston. Then ride

(R) north on Sheridan Road, sometimes on the sidewalk, sometimes on a separate bikeway. At the intersection of Sheridan and Greenleaf Street, a long stretch of separate bicycle path along the lake begins. At the sign for the scuba diving area, turn

(L) west onto Greenwood Street to the Dawes House of the Evanston Historical Society. Retrace path to bike path. As the bike path veers toward the lake and away from Sheridan Road, leave the path and turn

(L) west on Sheridan Road (ride on the sidewalk), then

(L) south on Chicago Avenue (ride on the sidewalk) to the national headquarters and birthplace of the Women's Christian Temperance Union. Retrace steps to the bike path. The separate path continues along the edge of the Northwestern University campus, past the astronomical observatory, and ends at Lincoln Street. Go

(L) west on Lincoln

(R) north and northwest on Sheridan Road, which then turns west. Almost immediately turn

(R) north, then west on Sheridan Place

(L) south on Sheridan Road for one block

(R) west on Isabella

(L) south on Woodbine

(L) east on Livingston

(R) south on Eastwood

(R) west on Central

(L) southeast on Green Bay Road (use the sidewalk). Just before the bridge over the North Shore Channel, turn

(R) west on bike path. The path proceeds through the Ladd Arboretum and ends at Emerson Street. Turn

(L) southeast on Emerson over the channel

(R) south as the bike path begins again. The path ends at Greenleaf, so turn

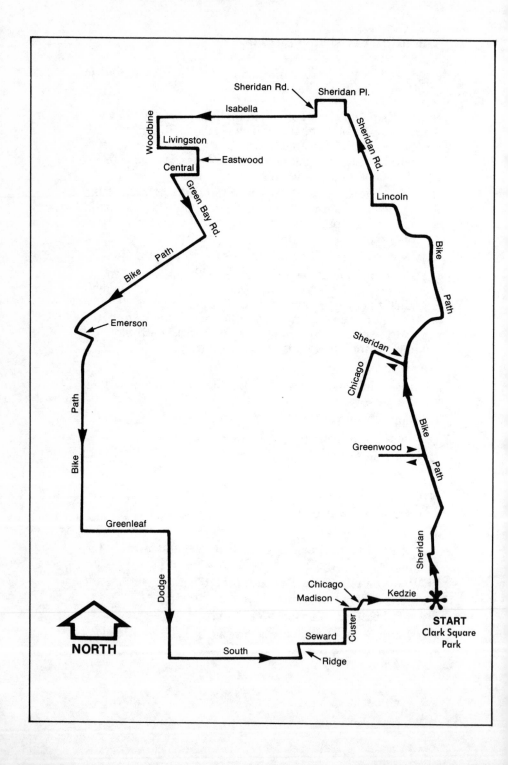

(L) east on Greenleaf
(R) south on Dodge
(L) east on South Boulevard. Jog
(L) north on Ridge Avenue when South becomes a one-way
street, then
(R) east on Seward
(L) north on Custer
(R) east on Madison. Jog
(L) north on Chicago Avenue. Immediately
(R) east on Kedzie, back to Clark Square Park.

The Baha'i Temple, Wilmette

Interurban Electric Terrain
Wilmette

Location:	Wilmette, 17 miles from downtown Chicago
Distance:	30 miles round trip
Traffic:	None on the trail; moderate to heavy on city streets
Camping:	None, but you can swim
Difficulty:	Easy
Riding time:	5–7 hours
Directions:	Take Lake Shore Drive north, then Sheridan Road north through Evanston to the corner of Linden Avenue in Wilmette.

Most of this ride is along the Green Bay Trail, a separate bike path which runs along the right-of-way of the late lamented North Shore Line, the Chicago and Milwaukee Electric Railroad, between Kenilworth and Highland Park. It's straight and level, and a half-dozen trim and shady parks are strung like beads along the route.

These are highly evolved suburbs in a way, with small "downtown" areas near the trail (as opposed to gigantic shopping malls).

There are unusual shops, restaurants, and places to

browse, and their commercial vitality depends on people who live nearby rather than people who have arrived straight out of an expressway chute.

We've stitched extensions onto both ends of the trail too. This ride begins in Wilmette at the center of the Baha'i faith in the United States, the Baha'i House of Worship at Sheridan and Linden.

The temple is a nonagon, made ethereal by vast expanses of glass and glorious, lacy concrete traceries inside and out. It is bordered by nine gardens and nine fountains. The temple is open to the public much of the time, but call for current schedules. Exhibits and slide shows in Foundation Hall explain the building and the faith.

A couple of doglegs to avoid traffic will carry you to the beach, which really bustles in the summer. Its thousand feet of shoreline offers sailboat rentals, sailing lessons, tennis, a fishing pier, picnic areas, and lifeguards. The route leaves the lake for the next several miles.

There's a friendly feeling about the Green Bay Trail, the next section of this ride. It begins with the notion that many people must have put imagination and long effort into the trail's creation.

On a sweltering summer day we came across a green rubber hose coiled neatly under a bush. Next to it was a hand-lettered sign marked Compliments of Bratschi Plumbing. Cool water too.

Not long after, we ducked into Harrie's Deli in Glencoe and asked the proprietor if it would be all right to buy just one cookie instead of a dozen. "Sure," he said. "And if you get tough with me, you can buy half a cookie."

Near the northern end of the trail were two uniformed, radio-equipped college-age cyclists of the mounted patrol of the Highland Park Police. The Green Bay Trail is part of their beat, they explained, and they are there to help lost children and overheated bikers and to check on reports of flashers or mishaps. That's friendly.

One destination on the northern extension of this ride, after you leave the trail in Highland Park, is the Jean Butz

James Historical Museum, which dates from 1871. Here you'll learn that Ravinia Park, which the trail passes, was launched by the electric railway as an amusement park to lure customers to the suburbs with "high-class vaudeville," a skating rink, and a toboggan slide. An early playbill listed Marguerite Sylva, "the Girl with the Auburn Hair"; Claude Gillingwater and Company; the Minstrel Maid; eight Bedouin Arabs; and others of equal prominence. Ravinia also had a stadium for outdoor sports, a music pavilion, a casino, a ballroom, and a theater that looked like a train station.

It is still the scene of the summer-long Ravinia Festival, of course. We heard an orchestra practicing somewhere behind the entrance gates as we tooled past on the return trip.

Another noteworthy landmark on the Highland Park section of the ride is the Francis Stupey log cabin in the city park, which dates from 1847 and is built of handhewn virgin timbers. It is the oldest standing structure in the town.

A Midwestern trait we all take for granted is "pride of place," and it is less common in regions with a more transient population. But it is here in the carefully restored Stupey cabin. Special trees more than 100 years old were sought out and found as far away as central Wisconsin when some of the timbers in this cabin were replaced. The white oak doors and windows were recrafted with wooden pegs and square nails.

The cabin was the Stupey family home from 1847 to 1875 and a farm building until 1896, when the farm was sold to the founders of the Exmoor Country Club. The club used it as a utility building until 1968, then gave it to the citizens of Highland Park. It was moved three-quarters of a mile to its present site and painstakingly restored.

Farther on is the entrance to Bronson Lake, then Rosewood Park and another welcome beach on Lake Michigan.

The Green Bay Trail is well marked for the most part but can be confusing. In general, remember that the path merges with Green Bay Road for short stretches, and that when the path forks, you should take the fork nearest the Chicago and North Western tracks.

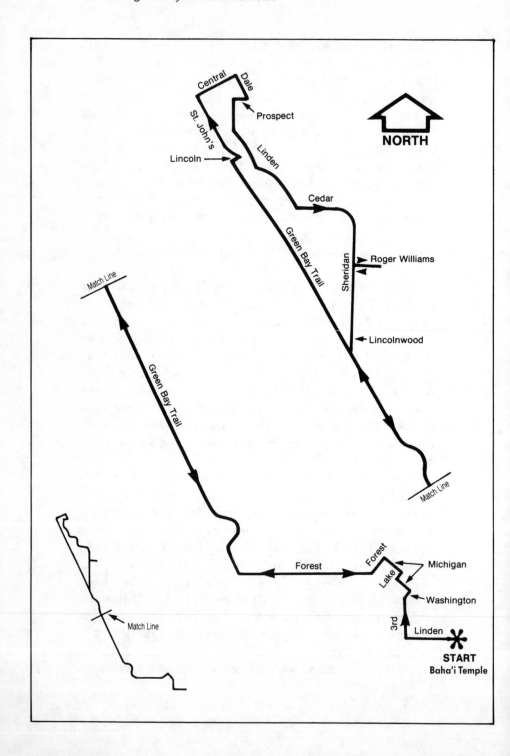

Interurban Electric Terrain

Start at the Baha'i Temple on Sheridan Road in Wilmette, just north of the Evanston city limits. Go

(R) west on Linden Avenue, away from Lake Michigan. Cross the North Shore Channel to

(R) north on 3rd. Cross Sheridan Road to Washington Beach and Park. From here, go

(L) northwest on Michigan Avenue, jog right briefly on Lake, then continue on Michigan to another beach. Pass the Michigan Shores Club, then go

(L) southwest on Forest Avenue. When it forks near Sheridan Road, take the right fork. Continue to the little playground on your right, across the street from the fire station. The sign says To Green Bay Trail, and that path is the beginning.

Some ten miles later, the trail ends in a large parking lot at Lincoln Avenue in Highland Park. Go north on St. John's Road from here, parallel to the trail. On your right you'll see the city hall and the Stupey cabin. Then turn

(R) east on Central, through the business district to the city historical museum. Then go

(R) south on Dale

(R) west on Prospect

(L) south on Linden. A park with an old-fashioned gazebo is on the right. Linden merges with Cedar, which veers

(L) east, then south when Cedar becomes Sheridan. Cross a creek, then go

(L) east on Roger Williams Avenue, past the entrance to Bronson Lake and to Rosewood Park and Beach. Turn around on Roger Williams and go

(L) south on Sheridan. Use the sidewalk because the street is too busy. Sheridan makes a right angle to the left, but we continue straight south as the road becomes Lincolnwood. Lincolnwood merges with St. John's. Go south on St. John's to the parking lot and rejoin the trail just inside the Glencoe city limits. Retrace path to the Baha'i Temple.

An old meeting hall along Ridge Road

Rock River Rendezvous
Grand Detour

Location:	Grand Detour, Illinois, about 85 miles west of Chicago
Distance:	46 miles round trip
Traffic:	Moderate; heavy near Lowden State Park and in the town of Oregon
Camping:	All varieties in both White Pines Forest State Park and Lowden State Park. Both parks are relatively unimproved, however, with flush toilets but no showers or water hookups. Lowden has electricity; White Pines does not.
Difficulty:	Moderately difficult
Riding time:	At least 6 hours
Directions:	Take the East-West Tollway (Illinois 5) west to the Dixon exit. Go north to the town of Dixon. In town, look for the signs for Illinois 2 heading northeast. Follow it to Grand Detour. You'll see the sign for the John Deere Historic Site from Illinois 2. There is plenty of parking in front of the site.

Who could be more midwestern than John Deere? His invention of the self-scouring plow literally opened up the prairie to cultivation. And now the company that bears his name is the largest manufacturer in Illinois.

Besides a dose of Deere biography, this ride takes you through the southernmost stand of white pines still in existence, the area where settlers clashed with Black Hawk, and a lovely former artists' colony on the banks of the Rock River.

The symbol of the agricultural Midwest was born and raised in Vermont. Fires destroyed his blacksmith shop there on two separate occasions, and business was bad. He, along with other Vermont residents, followed a countryman, Leonard Andrus, to a little village just laid out at a bend in Illinois's Rock River. Deere opened his blacksmith shop in the hamlet of Grand Detour.

Deere soon became involved in the problems of his friends and neighbors. Many of these first pioneers were quitting the area, deeply discouraged by their difficulties in plowing the thick, sticky prairie soil. The plows they brought from Vermont were engineered to cut through the sandy ground of that area. Here farmers had to stop every few steps and scrape the earth off their plows.

After experimenting with various shapes and sizes, Deere invented a self-scouring steel plow that cut through the soil smoothly and cleanly. His brainchild was an unqualified success, his business expanded rapidly, and in 1847 Deere moved to Moline, Illinois, to take advantage of better water transportation.

The 450 residents of Grand Detour, which means "big bend," proudly claim this spot as the "real" John Deere landmark, however. The railroad bypassed them, and Dixon, a bit to the south, became the county seat. Grand Detour, with its Greek Revival, Gothic, and Victorian homes, always maintained its nineteenth-century atmosphere except for its one big attraction, which draws 25,000 yearly.

The John Deere Historic Site, which includes John

*John Deere invented the "plough that broke the plains"
in Grand Detour.*

Deere's house, a replica of his blacksmith shop, a visitor
center, and a well-done archaeological exhibit showing the
exact spot where his shop and early plow factory stood, is
free. Guides give you short lectures on each building.

Your route passes through some of the farmlands that first
benefited from Deere's new plow and goes to White Pines

Forest State Park. A good place to take a prolonged rest, White Pines exudes peace. The Rock River twists and turns through the 385-acre preserve, and many trails skirt its moss-covered cliffs and venture into the forest.

Pines such as these used to cover much of northern Illinois, but this pristine stand is all that remains. Part of the reason is the white pines' usefulness. Used to construct ship masts, make matches, and help people with lung ailments, the trees were the first plants the Pilgrims saw when they reached America. Massachusetts manufactured wooden money from the tree and stamped it with a miniature white pine. The first settlers' houses were made from this sturdy tree.

The other state park on this ride is more famous for its connections with history than with botany. Lowden State Park boasts the 48-foot high statue of Black Hawk, standing 300 feet over the Rock River. The hollow statue weighs 100 tons, is reinforced with iron rods, and is from eight inches to three feet thick. It is the second largest concrete monolithic statue in the world.

Although the statue has been criticized as too idealized, it at least reminds visitors of the Indians who lived in and revered the valley before settlers drove them out. After losing the Black Hawk War, Black Hawk was quoted as saying: "Rock River was a beautiful country. I liked my towns, my cornfields, the home of my people. I fought for it—it is now yours—keep it, as we did."

The sculpture is the creation of Lorado Taft, one of the members of an artists' colony that gained inspiration from the scenic spot. The colony, which existed for fifty years, included author Hamlin Garland and noted musicians, scholars, writers, and artists from throughout the country. In its place is the Lorado Taft Field Campus, an outdoor laboratory for teacher education.

The town of Oregon, which you'll ride through, exhibits the works of the original artists' group in its public library at

300 Jefferson Street. There's an imposing courthouse on your route. Look for the soldiers' monument statue by Taft on the grounds. It's considered one of the best groupings of its kind. And if you enjoy shopping, check out Conover Square on North Third Street, a converted piano factory with a variety of shops and restaurants. Oregon hosts the Ogle County Fair in September, and the ride is particularly recommended during the fall, when color along the river is superb.

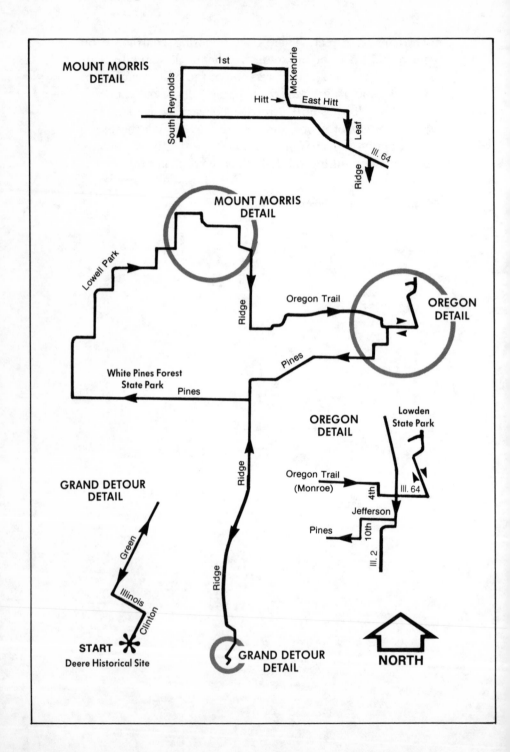

MOUNT MORRIS
DETAIL

1st

McKendrie

South Reynolds

Hitt

East Hitt

Leaf

Ill. 64

Ridge

MOUNT MORRIS
DETAIL

Lowell Park

Ridge

Oregon Trail

OREGON
DETAIL

Pines

White Pines Forest
State Park

Pines

Pines

OREGON
DETAIL

Lowden
State Park

Oregon Trail
(Monroe)

4th

Ill. 64

Jefferson

GRAND DETOUR
DETAIL

Pines

10th

Ill. 2

Green

Ridge

Illinois

Clinton

Ridge

START
Deere Historical Site

GRAND DETOUR
DETAIL

NORTH

Rock River Rendezvous

Start at John Deere Historical Site on Illinois 2 in Grand Detour. Go

(L) north on Clinton Street, which runs in front of the historical site
(L) west on Illinois Street
(R) north on Green Street, which becomes Ridge Road after it leaves town. Follow Ridge Road north to
(L) west on Pines Road, which can be quite busy, to White Pines Forest. Continue west on Pines Road to
(R) north on Lowell Park Road, which becomes South Reynolds Street as it enters Mt. Morris. Cross Illinois 64, then
(R) east on 1st Street
(R) south on McKendrie
(L) southeast on Hitt and almost immediately
(L) east on East Hitt across the tracks
(R) south on Leaf Road
(L) east on Illinois 64. Very soon after, turn
(R) south on Ridge Road
(L) east on the Oregon Trail into the town of Oregon, where it becomes Monroe Street
(R) south on North 4th
(L) east on Illinois 64 through town. Stay on the sidewalk if there's lots of traffic. Cross the Rock River and go
(L) north at the sign for the Taft Memorial. This road can be quite busy. Proceed until you see the sign for Lowden State Park on your left. Turn in at the sign. After the park, retrace path to Illinois 64 and turn
(R) west on Illinois 64
(L) south on Illinois 2 in the center of town
(R) west on Jefferson
(L) south on 10th
(R) west on Pines, which eventually merges to the left into Ridge Road. Continue south on Ridge Road to Grand Detour. Where it becomes Green Street, turn
(L) east on Illinois
(R) south on Clinton to the John Deere Historical Site.

*The belfry of the Blaine United Methodist Church,
built in 1860*

Capron Around
Boone County

Location:	Boone County, Illinois, about 70 miles northwest of Chicago
Distance:	About 30 miles
Traffic:	Light
Camping:	At Rock Cut State Park, 18 miles west
Difficulty:	Moderately difficult—a series of tough hills
Riding time:	5–7 hours
Directions:	Take Interstate 90 west, then north to its intersection with Illinois 173 near Rockford. Take 173 east to Capron, about 14 miles.

Weathered buildings, ruins, a buffalo wallow, some (literally) breathtaking hills and vivid local history characterize this ride near the Illinois-Wisconsin border.

The town of Capron was originally called Helgesaw, then Long Prairie. It was settled in the 1840s by a small colony of

Norwegian immigrants who were attracted by the availability of wood and water as well as farmland.

There were other settlers in the region by then, but they were few and the distances between them vast. The churches, cemeteries, and schoolhouses you'll see were gathering places for worship, deliberation, or celebration—bulwarks against the loneliness of the wide and empty prairie.

On September 30, 1873, Long Prairie was incorporated under its new name, Capron. It was said to be named after a Captain John Capron who helped get the Kenosha, Rockford, and Rock Island Railway (now the Chicago and North Western) to locate there in 1858. By that time the town had a population of 337, the largest in the area.

A high brick chimney marks the location of the K.K.O. Manufacturing Company in the southeastern section of Capron. The company makes restaurant equipment. Before 1958 the building was occupied by a commercial dairy. But when it was built a century ago, it was the cooperative Farmers' Friend Creamery.

On Fourth Street just south of Illinois 173 is the unusual Capron water tower (reminiscent of Chicago's but much larger), built over a well in 1900. The well is now 880 feet deep, and the tower still stores its 28,000 gallons, 90 feet above ground. It's easy to imagine the swelling pride of residents here when this still-elegant tower was constructed. Airmail pilots used it as a landmark on the Chicago-Minneapolis route in the thirties.

The following is a numbered guide to sites along the way. You can begin the ride at the school site in Capron, half a block north of Illinois 173 on Fourth Street.

1. A half-mile west of the intersection of Capron and Hunter roads is the location of a possible buffalo wallow, one of several said to be in the area, though there is no evidence that any of the settlers here ever saw a buffalo.

In 1837 Mr. Ormond Hayden was elected constable of this township because no one had a horse but Hayden rode a fast-trotting ox.

2. The small collection of buildings you'll find around the intersection of Blaine Road and Beaverton Road was once the thriving community of Blaine (see map for locations of buildings still standing).

   The first settlers arrived here in 1836 and homesteaded about a mile to the south, establishing the little cemetery you see on your left as you enter "town." The Blaine United Methodist Church across the road was built in 1860 for $1,195 by English immigrant stonemason Samuel Noble, and it is still in use.

   The former Blaine School is now a private home. Its predecessor was built of logs in 1857, and enrollment grew to fifty before the building was replaced with the present structure.

   The parsonage was built in 1863, the poorhouse was home for Blaine's underfinanced residents, and the present town hall was built on the site of an old cheese factory that burned down in the late 1890s.

3. The remains of another cheese factory can be seen on the south side of the road, just before the intersection of Blaine and Bergen roads. The considerable milk production in the county had to be processed immediately in the 1800s, before pasteurization and refrigeration, so small creameries, butter plants, and cheese factories were frequent. A brick chimney is all that remains of this one, and it has yielded bricks for fireplaces in several local homes.

4. A mile north on Grade School Road, after you turn off Blaine Road, is a house that stands at the site of the old Hamm's Tavern, a welcome stop on the stage route between Chicago and the Northwest in the mid-1800s. As

traffic grew, this establishment was added on to until it contained a dance hall, twenty sleeping rooms, a bar, and a kitchen "frequented by traders, soldiers, stage drivers, Indians, and other sorts of adventurers," according to the local historians from whom our information comes.

5. Next is Fish School, built in the 1840s and moved here to the intersection of Manchester and Grade School roads in 1850. Schools were also used for church services then—this was true of the Blaine School too—as well as other community activities.

6. At the top of this grade you can look out to the north into Wisconsin, whose border is a half-mile away. Watch your speed descending as there may be some sand on the road. You'll turn west along State Line Road, then head south again. Look out for a dog who lurks at this corner, and then look out for some real hills.

7. At the top of one of them is Forest Hill Cemetery, an excellent place to stop for a rest. Several Civil War veterans are buried here, along with many early settlers.

8. Manchester Free Church was organized in 1864. It has always been nondenominational, and visitors are welcome during the nine nonwinter months of the year that it is open. Farther south on Free Church Road, if you detour a mile east on Rockton Road, you can see a school built in 1866 in the now-vanished community of Bamlett, one of the earliest settlements in Boone County.

9. Gray School, near the corner of Free Church and Hunter roads, was built of limestone and thick timbers in 1858 so that it would last a long time. Its classes held forty-eight young'uns when school began in 1860.

10. *Kinnikinnick* is an alternative name for a low shrub sometimes called "bearberry," one of the components of the "tobacco" smoked by local Indians. On a bluff above Kinnikinnick Creek, near the conservation area, are the remains of a fourteen-foot-square cabin occupied by the Greenlee family in the 1850s.

11. The Livingston Cemetery was laid out in the early 1850s and contains the graves of several Civil War veterans. Also buried here was a sixteen-year-old boy who was struck by lightning while standing in the doorway of a barn. In an unsuccessful application of folk medicine, the boy was covered with earth to draw off the electric charge.

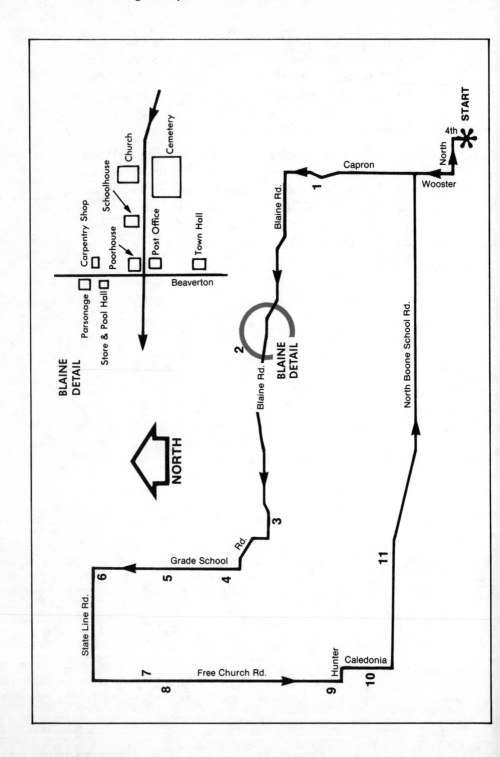

Capron Around

Begin at the Capron School site, one-half block north of Main Street (Illinois 173) on North 4th Street in Capron. Go north on 4th to

(L) west on North Street

(R) north on Wooster Street, which becomes Capron Road

(L) west on Blaine Road

(R) north on Grade School Road. Follow it as it jogs

(L) west and then

(R) north again

(L) west on State Line Road

(L) south on Free Church Road

(L) east on Hunter Road

(R) south on Caledonia Road. Kinnikinnick Creek Conservation Area is here, as are picnic tables. Then head

(L) east on North Boone School Road

(R) south on Capron Road

(L) east on North Street

(R) south on 4th to Start.

Chasing the Fox
Chain O'Lakes/Moraine Hills

Location:	60 miles north of Chicago, just south of Wisconsin
Distance:	46 miles, plus 11 miles of bike paths
Traffic:	Moderate; heavier on holidays and weekends
Camping:	Walk-in and car camping at Chain O' Lakes State Park
Difficulty:	Moderate
Riding time:	8–10 hours
Directions:	Take I-94 north, Illinois 173 west, Wilmot Road south, then left on Main Street/State Park Road to the park entrance.

The two state parks on this ride have the Fox River and their glacial origins in common, but much else about them is different. Chain O' Lakes was a Civilian Conservation Corps camp in the thirties and became a state park about twenty-five years ago. Moraine Hills is much newer; it was developed as a park in 1975.

Chain O' Lakes is open to motorboats, snowmobiles, and seasonal hunting. Only car-top boats without motors are allowed into Moraine Hills, and their use is severely restricted.

Moraine Hills is much smaller than Chain O' Lakes, but it embraces eleven miles of biking and hiking trails. Chain O' Lakes has only one 2½-mile nature trail.

At Chain O' Lakes you are much more likely to hear the throb of a bass guitar from someone's suitcase-sized transistor radio. At Moraine quieter forms of recreation are more in evidence.

Finally, Chain O' Lakes can have a worn-out, trashy look by mid-summer, while Moraine Hills, partly because it is newer and partly because it is maintained in a more natural state, is beautiful by comparison.

Bird watching is popular at Moraine Hills, and the Audubon Society has printed a free bird checklist, distributed at the park. It lists more than 100 species to watch for. Sadly, there is another checklist at the park interpretive center that includes thirty-three endangered species of birds in Illinois and another seven designated as threatened.

Another publication to pick up is the Pike Marsh Trail Guide, which takes you along an interpretive trail, pointing out what these marshes are made of and how they came to be this way. A highlight of the trail through Pike Marsh is a 1,300-foot boardwalk floating out over the murky water and through the cattails.

The lakes and marshes of the two state parks were formed when a receding glacier left big chunks of ice behind. As they melted, the meltwater formed a "kettle" which filled first with water, then with boggy plant material.

Pike Marsh exhibits several different kinds of plant communities, which vary depending on the light, water, and types of soil. There are several rare plants here, and the "largest known colony of pitcher plants in Illinois," according to a park brochure. These are carnivorous plants that trap bugs and "eat" them.

One delightful attribute of plants in Illinois is their names. Some names derive from early uses of the plant, its actual or supposed properties, a legend in which it plays a prominent role, or its appearance.

Here at Moraine Hills, on the lighter side, there are bladderwort, bog buckbean, joe-pye weed, sneezeweed, loosestrife, and meadowsweet. More sinister sounding are bloodroot, baneberry, nightshade, skullcap, and carrion flower, among others.

If you like to fish and have found a convenient method of carrying your pole and bait on your bike, both state parks offer a large variety of game fish. At McHenry Dam you can rent a boat and fish below the spillway.

An unusual feature of this ride is the connecting bike path from the McHenry Dam Recreation Area under the road to the main section of Moraine Hills.

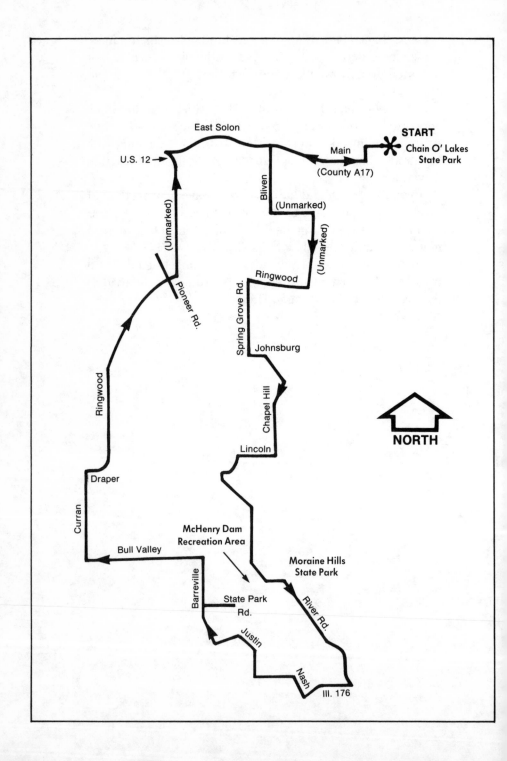

Chasing the Fox

Begin at Chain O' Lakes State Park's west entrance. Go west, then south on the main park road. Take the first road

(R) west. This is unmarked but is called Main Street and County A17. Continue west to Spring Grove, then

(L) south on Bliven, past Spring Grove Park, across U.S. 12

(L) east on the first unmarked road

(R) south on another unmarked road. Look for a house with a private lake and diving board. Turn

(R) west at Ringwood

(L) south on Spring Grove Road

(L) east on Johnsburg Road

(R) south on Chapel Hill Road, across the Fox River

(R) west on Lincoln Road to McHenry Dam Recreation Area, which is part of Moraine Hills State Park. Follow the bike path under Chapel Hill Road into the main section of the park and onto 11 miles of bike paths. Leave the park

(L) south on River Road

(R) west briefly on Illinois 176

(R) north on Nash Road along the river and bear left where the road forks

(R) north on Justin Road, which curves west

(R) north on Barreville Road

(R) east on State Park Road, if you want to go to the west bank of the Fox River. Otherwise continue north on Barreville to

(L) west on Bull Valley Road

(R) north on Curran Road

(R) east on Draper across Illinois 120. It turns north and becomes Ringwood Road. Cross Barnard Mill Road, railroad tracks, and Illinois 31, then turn

(L) north at the first unmarked road after Pioneer Road. Jog

(L) west briefly on U.S. 12, then

(R) east on East Solon Road, which becomes Main Street in Spring Grove. Return to Chain O' Lakes State Park.

Buffalo and bicyclist share a moment of mutual curiosity

Cornbelt Collage
Plano/Sandwich

Location:	56 miles west of Chicago near Aurora
Distance:	51.8-mile loop
Traffic:	Moderate; sometimes busy on Illinois 23
Camping:	Group camping only at Silver Springs State Park, future campsites planned for Shabbona Lake State Park
Difficulty:	Moderate
Riding time:	5–7 hours
Directions:	Take the East-West Tollway (Illinois 5) to Illinois 47. Turn south on 47, then west on U.S. 34 to Plano. Leave Plano south on Ben Street, which becomes the Fox River Road, and cross the Fox River to Silver Springs State Park.

When you're whizzing westward along the interstate, it looks as though the earth from Chicago to, roughly, Wyoming is nothing but flat and covered with cornstalks.

Wrong impression, as the cycle tourist knows. This ride, for instance, winds through an abundance of farm country

but also traverses the lovely Fox River Valley and includes
two historical and heavily wooded state parks, two herds of
buffalo, and even a camel! And that's just the beginning . . .

Silver Springs State Park is named for a bubbling spring
on its eastern end that never freezes over, even during the
coldest winters. The spring is on a nature trail that follows
the river to Loon Lake and a wildlife viewing area where
feeding deer, herons, ducks, and other animals can be seen.
The trail offers a good way to limber up just before or after
a long ride. A concession here rents canoes on weekends and
holidays from April to October.

The westernmost point on this tour is Shabbona Lake
State Park, named after a Potawatomi chief who refused to
join the Black Hawk War in the 1830s. He risked his life
instead to ride to the scattered farms of settlers throughout
the area and warn them of the danger.

Shabbona and Silver Springs have fishing for bass, bluegill,
crappie, sunfish, bullheads, tiger muskie, channel catfish, and
other species. Shabbona also has a fifteen-acre wildlife ref-
uge where several rare species of birds can be seen, especially during the migration period, which occurs from
around October 1 to January 1. Artificial Shabbona Lake,
within the park, covers 318 acres.

There's more history nearby. In the eighteenth century,
tribes of Sauk, Fox, Winnebago, and Potawatomi made alli-
ances with the rival European powers, Britain and France. A
force of Frenchmen and Indians surprised a group of three
hundred Fox at Maramech Hill, southeast of Plano, in 1730
and besieged them for more than three weeks. The Fox almost slipped through their encircling enemies on a stormy
night but were discovered at the last minute and killed.

More than a hundred years passed before the first major
settlement in the Plano area was established, in 1835, by a
group of Norwegian Quakers.

Bands of highwaymen, horse thieves, robbers, counterfeit-
ers, and other unsavories moved here, into DeKalb and Ogle

counties, as civilization pushed them westward. Around 1840, the evildoers more or less overwhelmed what there was of law and order. A group of outraged citizens, who called themselves "regulators," managed to terrorize the criminals and run them off with frontier justice until the law was firmly established.

Between Silver Springs and Sandwich you'll be on a road so free of traffic that all you have to watch out for is chickens. But these particular chickens share their homestead on one huge pasture with hogs, turkeys, sleepy Shetland ponies, cattle, burros, deer, several head of buffalo, goats, and at least one camel (in a pen next to the road).

This part of Illinois must be congenial for buffalo. A herd of twenty or so romp on a big farm you'll pass between Plano and Little Rock. In spring you can see their enormous, woolly, but still endearing offspring. Look for this herd where you see the sign saying Honey for Sale—Next Farm. Sometimes these animals, with deep brown eyes as big as cue balls, may mosey over to the fence to take a look at passing bicyclists. Curious, but immensely dignified.

In Sandwich, named after Sandwich, Massachusetts, look for the faded, amazing art deco diner on your right as you enter from the south. The edge of town in Sandwich is abrupt: a tree-lined street with suburban-looking houses suddenly stops at a cornfield stretching almost to the horizon. If you turn your head over your shoulder as you pedal north out of Sandwich, you can see the water tower—the symbol of "town" in the Midwest—and up ahead one of the tallest old windmills—the symbol of farm life anywhere. And from there to Shabbona, it's all farm. A gathering of cars may indicate a family reunion or a country auction.

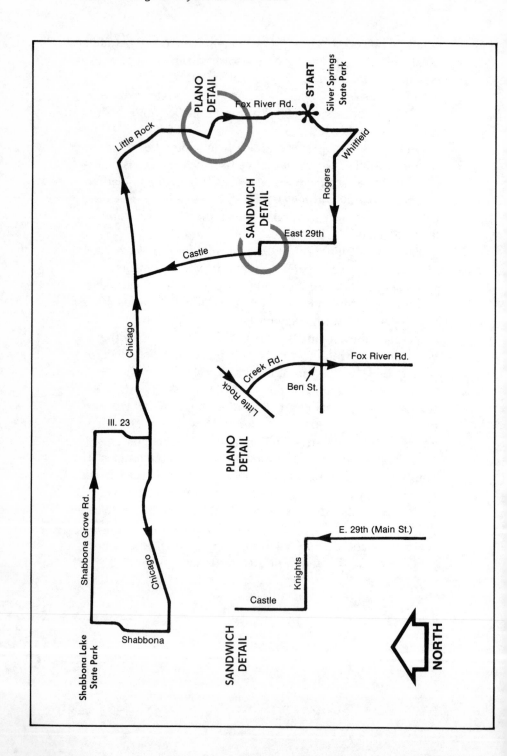

Cornbelt Collage

Start this ride at Silver Springs State Park. Turn

(L) south on Fox River Road. Curve right through a wildlife management area, then go

(R) north on Whitfield Road. The camel is here. Cross the river, and head

(L) west on Rogers Road

(R) north on East 29th Road, which becomes Main Street in town. When you cross Railroad Avenue, you can detour right a couple of blocks to see the old city hall, built in 1870. Then

(L) west at Sandwich Hospital, onto Knights Road

(R) north on Castle Road. When pavement ends, go

(L) west on Chicago Road, past the Oak Mound Cemetery and across Illinois 23

(R) north on Shabbona Road

(R) east on Shabbona Grove Road. Enter the state park through two stone pillars. The entrance is closed to auto traffic. After leaving Shabbona Lake State Park, you'll pass through the hamlet of Shabbona Grove. Turn

(R) south on Illinois 23

(L) east on Chicago Road to Little Rock Road

(R) south on Little Rock

(L) east and south on Creek Road, which becomes Ben Street in Plano. South of Plano, Ben Street becomes Fox River Road and returns you to Silver Springs State Park.

Waterway

Starved Rock

Location:	Across the Illinois River from the town of Marseilles, about 60 miles southwest of Chicago
Distance:	37 miles
Traffic:	Moderate; heavy in state parks on weekends
Camping:	In Starved Rock and Illini state parks, both trailers and tents
Difficulty:	Moderate, a few hills
Riding time:	6 hours, but plan to linger in the parks
Directions:	Take I-80 west to the Marseilles exit; go through town and over the bridge to Illini State Park.

Campers at Illini State Park are sometimes wakened by mournful air horns or by the basso throbbing of a big towboat as it pushes barges along the Illinois River. Compared to high-balling semis on the interstate, or even to freight trains, it all may seem lethargic, even outdated.

But it's a busy river, and each one of those barges moves as much freight (1,500 tons) as fifteen jumbo railroad hopper cars or sixty trucks. They are often lashed together in blocks of eight or nine barges each, and at the beginning of this ride visitors can watch these gargantuan loads of coal or soybeans or gravel ease past a twenty-six-foot drop in the river at the Marseilles Lock.

The lock doesn't attract crowds, but it's awesome. Two huge pairs of gates enclose 22 million gallons of water. Barge blocks are nudged into the lock past the downriver gates and lifted upward by the water to proceed on their way toward Chicago; or they're going downriver, toward the Mississippi, and are lowered to the new river level as water is released from the lock.

There are 7,000 of these lockages at Marseilles each year, and the process goes on twenty-four hours a day. In midwinter ice is broken in and around the lock to keep the traffic moving. Marseilles's is only one of eight lock-and-dam combinations regulating the 333 miles of the Illinois River between Lake Michigan and the Mississippi, and together they stairstep boats and barges over a 160-foot change in water level.

As you pedal away from Marseilles, watch for a house with an amazing collection of whirligigs in the front yard, a proud old barn with 1898 in big wooden numerals under its eaves, a long look out over the river valley as the road climbs a ridge, a tiny town hall and its outhouse almost lost in a sea of corn . . .

The route leads away from the river and through the outskirts of Ottawa, then on to historic Starved Rock State Park. Here you can give your posterior a rest by hiking several trails through eighteen striking canyons that cleave thick beds of sandstone. In summer the park has a good program of guided hikes and nature movies on Saturday nights.

Starved Rock itself is a 125-foot sandstone butte overlooking the river. Legend has it that a group of Illinois Indian warriors was trapped on the rock and starved during a battle with the Ottawa and Potawatomi.

The French built Fort St. Louis atop the rock from 1682 to 1683 in order to gain strategic control over the river. The fort was also to be a link in a chain of forts to halt British expansion toward the Mississippi Valley.

If you're spending more than a day on this ride or planning to camp overnight, Starved Rock is a larger and more beautiful place than Illini, so start and end your ride with this in mind.

Flying squirrels live here, as well as yellow-bellied sapsuckers (birds that leave neatly drilled lines of little holes in the bark of cedar trees), salamanders, and rock doves. For more information on flora and fauna, pick up the excellent park brochure.

Watch yourself on the winding roads of this park. They're distractingly beautiful, but traffic can be brisk, the hills are steep, the shoulders are eroded and narrow, and the road has cracks as of this writing. If you want more than a glance, it's probably best to dismount.

At the western border of the park is Illinois 178. It's not part of this route but if traffic is light and you haven't had your fill of locks and dams, you may want to brave the slender sidewalk and go over the bridge, turning right on Dee Bennett Road (it can also be trafficky) for about a mile and a half to the Illinois Waterway Visitor Center.

The center offers a well-crafted series of exhibits on the history and development of the river and includes fascinating information on the locks and how they work. On the river side of the building is the Starved Rock Lock and Dam, and you can get a panoramic view of its operations from the roof.

Until 1947 the public could walk across the dam to this side of the river. If they ever open it up again, we can all get to the visitor center from the state park on our bikes! Write your state representatives and senators.

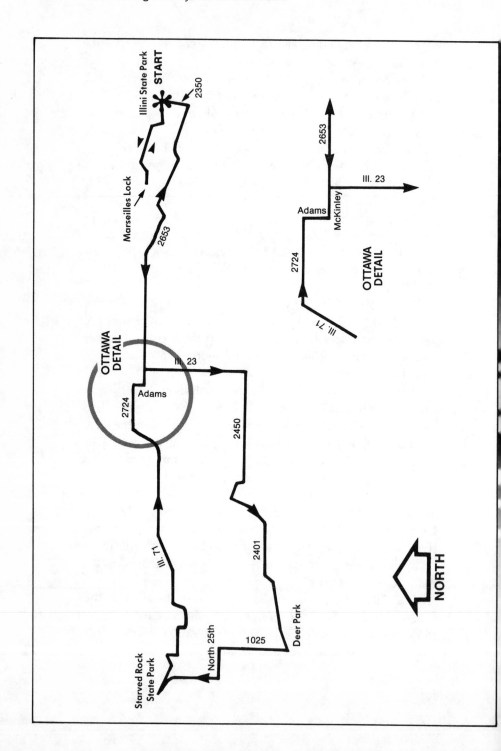

Waterway

Pedal 2½ miles along the partly paved downriver road leading away from Illini State Park headquarters to the Marseilles Lock; return the same way, then out the park's main
entrance and

(L) south on county road 2350 (a sometimes busy, narrow
     road)
(R) west on 2653, all the way to Ottawa. When you see the
     shopping mall on your left, turn
(L) south on Illinois 23
(R) west and northwest on 2450
(L) west on 2401
(R) north at Deer Park on 1025
(L) west at North 25th
(R) north at the first road
(L) west to Starved Rock State Park entrance
(R) east on Illinois 71
(R) east on 2724 past 4-H grounds and an old artesian well
(R) south on Adams
(L) east on McKinley, which becomes 2653 outside of town
(L) north on 2350 back to Illini State Park.

A Two-Wheeler Towpath
Gebhard Woods

Location: 45 miles southwest of Chicago in the
                town of Channahon

Distance: 34 miles round trip

Traffic: Nonexistent—separate bicycle and hiking
                path

Camping: Tent camping only at Gebhard Woods
                State Park; other camping 17 miles west
                at Illini State Park

Difficulty: Easy, but trail rough in spots because of
                hard-packed gravel surface

Riding time: 4–6 hours; allow more time because of
                gravel

Directions: Take I-55 southwest to I-80 west. At the
                Channahon exit turn south to U.S. 6.
                The trail begins off U.S. 6 at a marked
                parking area near the town of
                Channahon.

Looking at the placid waters of the Illinois and Michigan
Canal as it flows gently through cool forests and along the

back edges of small towns, it's hard to imagine that this modest waterway is largely responsible for the commercial development of Chicago and, indeed, the entire northeast portion of Illinois. But that's why it's on the National Register of Historic Places, why historians have written treatises about it, why historical markers herald it, and why it's now preserved as a bicycle and hiking path.

The canal's history began about 8,000 years ago when an ancient river carved a path for it. Before the state of Illinois began constructing the canal, before there even was a state of Illinois, Indians made the former riverbed deeper by carrying goods from the waters of Lake Michigan across low land to the Des Plaines River. This path, called the Chicago Portage, was recorded by the French explorers Joliet and Marquette in 1673.

When the canal was first conceived in 1820, Chicago was a village of only a dozen houses. By the canal's completion in 1848, over 12,000 people lived there. The canal began showing a profit almost immediately, and within months of its opening Chicago's population jumped to 20,000. In the next decade the city quadrupled in size. The ninety-mile waterway, which ran all the way from Chicago to La Salle, Illinois, and provided the link between the Great Lakes and the Mississippi River, was the main reason for this growth. By the 1870s, when the stench of sewage dumped from Chicago became too much for boat passengers and forced the canal's decline, Chicago was a powerful city in its own right.

Today, in the zenith of a midsummer afternoon, the thick curtains of walnut, oak, cottonwood, and ash trees make a shady, deep-green arbor and also give protection from occasionally powerful prairie winds. Red and purple mulberries carpet the ground in season.

Imagine the canal side of the trail barren of trees. Mules and horses once moved along the seventeen-foot-wide path, pulling boats and barges along, so the towpath had to be kept clear of any vegetation. Packet boats, about the size of a modern city bus, would haul full loads of ninety people on the twenty-five-hour trip from Chicago. The "luxury" trip cost four dollars and was considered the most pleasant way to travel, despite the fact that passengers were not allowed to open any windows for fear of catching malaria from the swarms of mosquitoes. The packet boats and the freight barges made for a busy, if slow-moving, passage.

As you ride the first several miles of the trail west from Channahon, try to visualize the canal as it once was. The trail runs between this deserted, watery backroad and the Illinois River, a bustling, nautical superhighway that in one year accommodates barge loads totaling 44.5 million tons of coal, grain, chemicals, and other products. You may see barges, some from as far away as New Orleans, as they use thick ropes to tie up to trees along the path, waiting to go through the Dresden Island lock.

All this water means mosquitoes are thick, so add repellent to your checklist. The gravel is soft in spots, crisscrossed with large ruts in a few others, and there are some enormous chuckholes. This makes for slower, more careful riding. And, although most of the trip transports you decades away from the twentieth century, there are a few reminders, like the spaceship domes of the Dresden Nuclear Power Plant across the river, or brief, pungent smells from nearby factories.

These features of the ride are not all drawbacks. The chuckholes often reveal fat, furry rodents—muskrats, beavers, and squirrels—especially in early evening.

Hills? This ride doesn't have them. Curves are few and usually take you over a bridge, along an aqueduct, or across a road. Fishing is a favorite activity. Bass, bluegill, and crappie are the most plentiful fish. The path runs through state parks—Channahon, McKinley Woods, Gebhard Woods, and William G. Stratton—and there are several quiet picnic spots.

Graceful old canal locks, a restored stone aqueduct, the old lockkeeper's house, and some tall red-brick buildings, some of which used to be the headquarters for the William Gebhard Brewery operation in the late 1800s, are all visible from the trail. Old Gebhard beer bottles have been found along the towpath too.

If you look sharply, you'll see a sign marked Grave. It points the way to Chief Shabbona's final resting place. An even more obscured feature is farther down the trail: the largest cottonwood tree in Illinois is hidden in these woods. It's one mile west of the Gebhard Woods parking lot. Cross the aqueduct and follow the path. The tree is not marked, but at 120 feet high with a circumference of 27 feet 4 inches and a crown spread of 111 feet, it's hard to miss.

Plan on returning in a year or two because this bike path will eventually stretch from Joliet in the east to La Salle in the west, a distance of sixty-one miles.

Start your ride at the Illinois and Michigan Canal parking area near the town of Channahon, just off U.S. 6. Residents say fishing is good along this portion of the canal and the Illinois River, so bring your pole. The trail passes through the unmarked McKinley Woods State Park, then on to William G. Stratton Park in the town of Morris. The aqueduct and the trail to the largest tree start between Stratton and the trail's terminus at Gebhard Woods State Park.

INDIANA

Tree Trek
Crown Point/Lemon Lake

Location:	Crown Point, Indiana, 24 miles south of Gary
Distance:	33 miles round trip
Traffic:	Moderate, with two brief exceptions
Camping:	None
Difficulty:	Moderate
Riding time:	5–6 hours
Directions:	Take I-90 east from Chicago through Hammond and Gary to I-65 south. Take U.S. 231 exit west and north into the outskirts of Crown Point, then left (south) at the signal on Indiana 55. Take the first left onto South Street and turn into the parking lot by the Hub Pool at the end of the block.

As midwestern pioneers gradually and painfully improved from impoverished sodbusters to solid citizens with a little capital, the civic-minded among them often tried to create the "ideal town." One big decision, weighed very carefully because it helped determine the character of a place, was what kind of trees would be planted.

Trees are still the glory of many of these communities a century and more later, and if you get the feeling in larger cities at times that "something's missing" from business districts and residential areas alike, it's often the trees.

Take no offense if you're a bird watcher, please, but tree watching is just as appealing and a lot easier. On this ride (as on most of the others in this book) cyclists can see the native species that town fathers had to choose from and some of the imported varieties too. They don't hide or hop around or fly away, and they don't migrate. They're standing around out there, waiting to be observed and appreciated.

Two lovely and comparatively little-used county parks are included on this ride. You may want to leave your bike and take a stroll to see how many trees you can identify. To help with your tree watching, here's a short list of species with their identifying features that can be seen at Stony Run Park.

Black walnut (*Juglans nigra*)—grows only in the United States and is said to be one of our most valuable trees. Its roots give off a poisonous substance, jugalone, which kills most other plants that would normally grow beneath it. Prized for its beautiful, hard wood that is used in fine furniture, gunstocks, and similar products. Grows up to 150 feet high throughout the Midwest in deep soil. Each leaf stem has thirteen to twenty-five leaflets with fine-toothed edges, and each leaflet is one to two inches long. The walnuts are for eating, and the tough green husks yielded a brown dye for the pioneers.

Slippery elm (*Ulmus rubra*)—less common here, forty to seventy feet high, has reddish-brown or gray bark covering a slippery inner bark used in bygone days to prevent scurvy. Serrated, thick leaves, four to seven inches long, taper to a

slender point from an oval-shaped main section. Paler underneath. Red blossoms in spring and reddish, fuzzy twigs in
spring and fall.

Pignut hickory (*Carya glabra*)—hickory nuts are usually
bitter but edible; the wood is used for smoking meats and
making tool handles and hunting bows. Member of the walnut family. Eight- to twelve-inch leaves usually made up of
five finely serrated fragrant leaflets. Dark gray bark with
grooves on the trunk. Male flowers or "catkins" hang in
threesomes.

Shagbark hickory (*Carya ovata*)—eight- to fourteen-inch
leaves with five leaflets, last leaflet the largest. The gray bark
curls off the trunk, looks "shaggy." Nuts sometimes sweeter,
used to produce barbecue briquettes. Was important in making wagon wheels.

White, red, and black oaks (*Quercus alba, rubra, velu-
tina*)—white oaks sometimes live for 600 years, have whitish
bark and leaves with seven to nine round lobes. These trees
are sometimes wider at the top than they are high.

Red oaks have thick, near-black bark with red inner bark;
leaves have little pointed tips on the end of each lobe. There
are from seven to eleven lobes, sinuses go halfway to the
mid-rib, and the leaves are light green except in the fall,
when they turn red and orange.

Black oak leaves have hairy undersides, five to seven lobes,
and elongated, curving points on their tips; sinuses go two-
thirds to seven-eighths of the way to the mid-rib. The bark is
dark outside and yellow or orange underneath.

Black willow (*Salix nigra*)—grows in wet soil, appears as
both a drooping waterside bush and a full-fledged tree with
black bark and branches. Green, slender leaves with fine
serrations, three to six inches long.

Black cherry (*Prunus serotina*)—less common. The fine-
grained wood is used for cabinets and veneer. Leaves are
egg-shaped with slightly flattened sides, they have little red
hairs at the base, uniform serrations, and they smell like

Red Oak Leaf

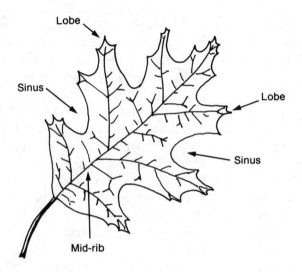

bitter almonds. Bears white blossom clusters in April and May. Cherries are small, red or black, and have a winelike taste. The black cherry has gray bark. Old trees have bark with upturned edges.

If you'd like more information on tree identification, check out George A. Petrides's *Field Guide to Trees and Shrubs* (Boston: Houghton Mifflin, 1973).

Crown Point has some lovely tree-lined streets. It also boasts, on its busy downtown square, an imposing court-house, one of the largest buildings attempted by settlers of that time (1878) in the area. Its design is a blend of Georgian, Victorian, and Romanesque styles, and it is tall enough to be seen at a great distance over its relatively flat surroundings. A morainic divide gives the building part of its uplift. Rivers north of the divide flow into the St. Lawrence River system, and those south of it flow into the Mississippi.

Glaciers covered this area during their Ice Age advances, which began about a million years ago and lasted until about 20,000 years ago. This moraine was formed when glacial debris—ground-up rock and soil—was deposited by the Lake Michigan Ice Lobe as it retreated northward.

A tempting side trip, at least on the map, can be made to Cedar Lake near Lemon Lake Park. The narrow roads around the lake are very busy with cars and trucks, however, and its perimeter is chock-a-block with houses, save for a dusty lot that serves as a launch ramp and a small and forlorn city park on a near-squalid (as of this writing) strip of lakefront.

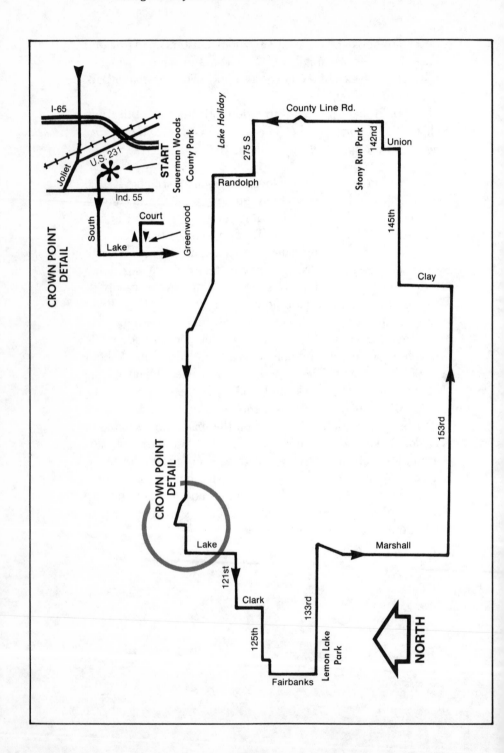

Tree Trek

Start in Crown Point, Indiana, at Sauerman Woods County Park. Go out past the pool, then turn

(L) west on South Street. Cross Indiana 55. Turn

(L) south on Lake Street.

> If you want to swim or picnic here, you can detour left on Greenwood, then right on Court (use sidewalk because of traffic) to the county fairgrounds. There are picnic tables, a lake, and a covered bridge here. Retrace your path to Lake Street. Turn south on Lake, then

(R) west on 121st

(L) south on an unmarked road, which you'll later learn is Clark. The road is the second one that goes to the left. Turn

(R) west on 125th

(L) south, then west, then south again on Fairbanks

(L) east on 133rd to the entrance to Lemon Lake County Park. There's picnicking and paddle boat rentals here. After the park, continue east on 133rd. Go straight where the road curves left at the stop sign, then

(R) south on Marshall Road

(L) east on 153rd, where Marshall Road ends

(L) north on Clay Road, where 153rd ends

(R) east on 145th. Continue straight across railroad tracks, then

(L) north as the road curves (and becomes Union Road)

(R) east on 142nd to entrance of Stony Run Park. As you leave the park, going east on 142nd, turn

(L) north on County Line Road. When you come to a sharp left turn, turn right instead and cross the railroad tracks; turn left on the road just across the tracks, which then curves and continues north. When County Line ends, go

(L) west on 275S, past Lake Holiday

(R) north on Randolph

(L) west at sign for Camp LRCA. Follow the road over Interstate 65 to the stop sign immediately after the railroad tracks. Turn slightly

(R) west and a bit north on Joliet Street, about ¼ mile to the
signal

(L) south on Indiana 55

(L) east on South Street and return to Sauerman Woods
County Park.

The Amish
Nappanee

Location:	About 100 miles from Chicago in northern Indiana
Distance:	32 miles
Traffic:	Light
Camping:	None
Difficulty:	Easy
Riding time:	5–7 hours
Directions:	Take I-94 east, then south on U.S. 421 between Gary and Michigan City. Go east on U.S. 6 to Amish Acres, just west of Nappanee.

Distinguishing an Amish farm from others on this ride is partly a matter of looking for what isn't there. No electric wires, no automobiles or motorized farm equipment, no TV antennas.

It doesn't involve guesswork, though, when you see a black buggy or two parked in a side yard or a bearded farmer cultivating behind a draft horse. Your chances are excellent of seeing and not-seeing the quality of Amish life over your handlebars here.

About 2,500 Amish people live in the area, and there are many more in northern Indiana. Their most striking characteristic is a tenacious religious devotion to simplicity in dress, in labor, in worship, and in manner of living, as a means of remaining close to God. In practical terms, this concern translates into living on the land as farmers, using draft animals rather than motorized machines for farm work and transportation, and dressing in the fashion of their ancestors of a century or two ago.

Amish families are not completely insulated from modern life. They read newspapers to keep up with world events, and indeed they are surrounded by insistent evidence of the way the rest of us live. Within their society are subtle degrees of adaptation to passing time. These grow out of differing opinions on what innovations can be incorporated into Amish lives without making them more complex and less spiritual. One group uses rubber-lined wheels on its buggies, for example, while another does not allow them.

Some few Indiana Amish speak Swiss, but most use three other languages: "Pennsylvania Dutch," which is not Dutch at all but a High German dialect much like Rhinelanders still use in Germany; English, for contact with the "English" people of the outside world; and High German, for worship and other ceremonial activities connected with religion, such as hymn singing and Bible reading.

Look for a small cemetery left of the road as you enter Wakarusa. Its diminutive white gravestones reflect the Amish belief that all are equal in the sight of God and that pride and ostentation are sinful.

The Amish reliance on horse-drawn transportation and farm implements supports a variety of occupations that are now antiquated in our culture. You'll see a harness maker's shop on this ride, and there are also blacksmiths and carriage makers in the area. In spring and fall you'll see those horses at work in the fields.

Amish farming is productive as well as frugal. The soils on their farms have been found to be better maintained and much freer of pollutants than land farmed by contemporary methods. Productivity is high (though the work is hard!) and, in our terms, the farms are prosperous, partly because so little is spent on "luxury" and partly because the farms are well managed.

Much else could be said of the Amish, but the price of generalizations is that they are always untrue to some degree. At Amish Acres, where this ride begins, there are guided tours of eighteen restored buildings, including a twelve-room Amish farmhouse, which illustrate how the Amish live and what they believe. Less expensive and quite informative is a half-hour movie, *Beyond the Buggy*, which costs a dollar to see.

Bicycle touring is especially appropriate here. The efficient simplicity of your nonmotorized bike seems less intrusive as you ride past the clean, quiet farms. You may see, as we did, friendly cyclists on these roads, many with children, but dressed in bonnets and long, pleated skirts or black cloth coats and wide-brimmed hats. These Amish cyclists share, in a kind of cultural kinship, the same idea you have.

In at least one Amish area in Illinois separate traffic lanes have been set aside for buggies to travel safely. But there are none around Nappanee, so be alert when you're driving and pass slowly. Many Amish people do not like to be photographed. Probably most would not like being quizzed about themselves, any more than you and your family would if strangers were pedaling through your neighborhood, even if the curiosity were fervently well intentioned. Some Amish people, on the other hand, enjoy conversation with outsiders. So use your good judgment.

There is much to be said for the non-Amish section of this ride too, including sleepy Wakarusa, home of the Bird's Eye

Amish man pedals along the road to Nappanee

Museum. Unheralded except for the name on the mailbox on the left side of South Elkhart Avenue as you enter town, the museum is in a private home. Inside is one of the largest collections of miniature buildings in the world, made of toothpicks, popsicle sticks, cratewood, rusty wire, and steel wool. More than 4,000 hours went into the creation of these one-inch to five-foot scale models.

Just east of the business district, next to the firehouse, is a good rest stop: a vest-pocket park shaded by the homely magnitude of the Wakarusa water tower. You can have a snack at the sole picnic table and wait, perhaps, for a fire drill.

But don't wait too long. A couple of blocks away is a historical museum in a former train depot. Again, the sign is small, but you may see an old steam tractor out in front.

The Society to Save the Wakarusa Depot was formed in 1975, according to President Helen Klein, and the building was moved after a community fund-raising effort. The depot and a smaller building adjacent to it contain some old railroad antiques, the first Iron Lung in Elkhart County, a nineteenth-century printing press, quilts, plates, fire-fighting equipment, the last oil-burning street lamp (1908), and many other items.

The depot was moved to the present site by the huge steam tractor, which may be next to the depot when you visit, right next to an old wooden caboose. "Most of Wakarusa walked with the building on a fall day," writes Ms. Klein. "It was a beautiful sight. The tractor stopped to fill up with water one time. All the newspapers covered the story."

The two museums do not have regular hours, but if you call Ms. Klein at (219) 862-4407 or 862-2825 and let her know when you'll be in Wakarusa, she may be able to tell you when they will be open or arrange to have them open for you.

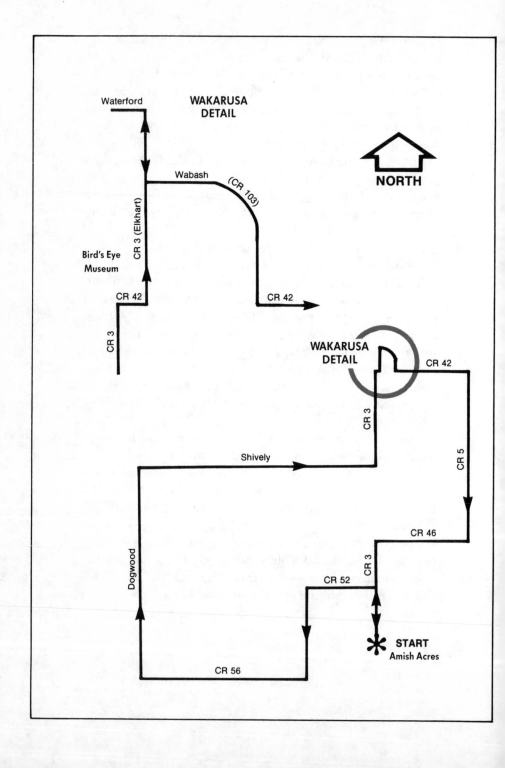

The Amish

Begin at Amish Acres tourist attraction just west of Nappanee, Indiana. Go

(R) north on CR 3, which runs along the west side of Amish Acres

(L) west on CR 52, past the Maple Lawn Church

(L) south at the first paved road, past the United Christian School, and across U.S. 6

(R) west on CR 56 (heavy concentration of Amish farms here)

(R) north on Dogwood Road

(R) east on Shively Road

(L) north on CR 3. Jog

(R) east on CR 42, then continue

(L) north on CR 3 into Wakarusa. This becomes Elkhart Street in town. Watch for the Bird's Eye Museum on your left, then turn

(L) west one block on Waterford Street to see horse-drawn hearses. Return to Elkhart Street. The water tower is near the corner of Harrison and Elkhart. Go

(L) east on Wabash Street (CR 103), which curves south as it leaves town. Watch for the museum just before crossing the railroad tracks, then

(L) east on CR 42

(R) south on CR 5

(R) west on CR 46

(L) south on CR 3. Watch for harness shop on your left. Then return to Amish Acres.

Battleground
Tippecanoe River Country

Location: Indiana, 95 miles southeast of Chicago

Distance: 46 miles

Traffic: Light to moderate; briefly heavy in Monticello

Camping: Several private car campgrounds at Indiana Beach

Difficulty: Moderate

Riding time: 6–8 hours

Directions: Take I-90 to Gary, then I-65 south. Turn onto Indiana 43 north exit. After 1½ miles, take the Indiana 225 turnoff east and south to the town of Battleground.

They still find musket balls buried in the bark of old trees at the site of the Battle of Tippecanoe. The feeling that the old trees were present at a turning point in history is preserved here 170 years later.

Monuments and exhibits at the site, now a state historical park, recount the grim buildup of hostilities between the Indians of the Wabash Valley and settlers in what had been part of Canada until the Revolutionary War. We look back on the conflict from a safe distance as the collision of two ways of life with competing, contradictory, and irreconcilable claims on the land.

In 1792 Major General George St. Clair of the United States Army and 600 of his soldiers were killed at the headwaters of the Wabash, a defeat so embarrassing that President George Washington at first refused to let a congressional investigating committee see any correspondence on the incident. It was the first time in U.S. history that the doctrine of executive privilege was invoked. Washington said it would be harmful for the public to hear the details of the defeat.

Conflicts between Indians and settlers in Kentucky, Indiana, and Illinois continued. On the largely unmarked maps of the time, Chicago was just a small X in the wilderness between Qoshqonong and Grand Kickapoo Village.

One of the young Shawnee warriors present at some of the battles of that time was Tecumseh. Twenty years later he was the master military strategist for an alliance of Indian tribes that he and his brother, the Prophet, had organized to resist white encroachment.

At the Battle of Tippecanoe, November 7, 1811, Indian forces led by the Prophet attacked the military encampment of William Henry Harrison, governor of Indiana Territory and later president of the United States. The Indian alliance was routed, and the dream of Indian dominance east of the Great Plains was broken.

The distance from Chicago to Battleground and from Chicago to Monticello is about the same, so you could begin at either end of this ride. Just be sure, as always, to travel in the direction indicated on the map, so the road signs you see will match it.

Monticello is a resort town whose economic prospects began looking up about fifty years ago when dams were built on the Tippecanoe and Lakes Shafer and Freeman formed. Another drawing card is the Indiana Beach amusement park. We couldn't sketch a bike route there because the roads are too congested. The route does include a swimming beach in Monticello, however.

We were delighted to come across Bicycle Bridge Road way out in the back country. There may be some interesting local legend behind this name, but we figured it was chosen because the old bridge that carries the road over the Tippecanoe is so slender that only bicycles can use it at the same time without colliding.

The Tippecanoe, which runs clear much of the time, joins the perpetually turbid Wabash just a mile or so south of the point where Tyler Road branches off Main Street in Battleground. It was at the junction of these two rivers that Tecumseh and the Prophet established a headquarters village.

The battlefield site has a new and well-thought-out interpretive exhibit. Each year, on two weekends around the Fourth of July, there is a gathering of Indiana fiddlers and other traditional musicians. Also held in summer are the Battlefield Art Festival and Tippecanoe Lodge Pow Wow.

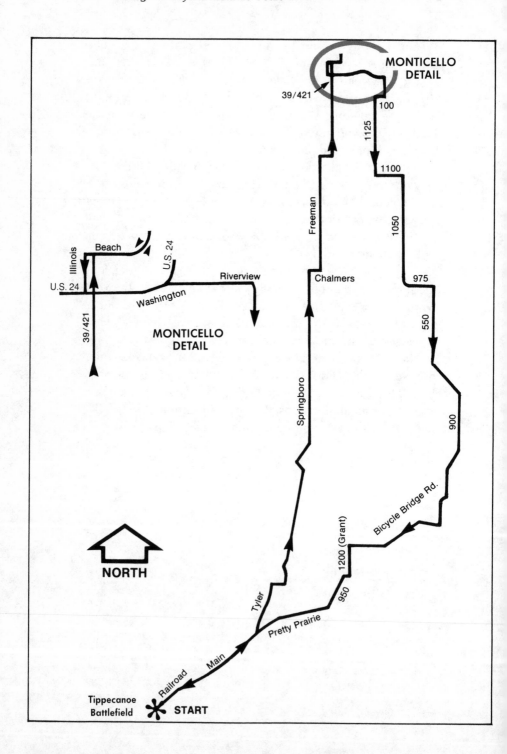

MONTICELLO DETAIL

100

1125

1100

Freeman

1050

Chalmers

975

550

39/421

Beach

Illinois

U.S. 24

U.S. 24

Riverview

Washington

39/421

MONTICELLO DETAIL

Springboro

900

Bicycle Bridge Rd.

1200 (Grant)

950

NORTH

Tyler

Pretty Prairie

Main

Railroad

Tippecanoe
Battlefield

START

Battleground

Start this ride at the Tippecanoe Battlefield State Memorial parking lot, ½ mile southeast of the town of Battleground on Railroad Street. From the parking lot, go

(L) north on Railroad Street, leaving the battlefield

(R) northeast on Main Street, to a Y in the road

(L) north on Tyler Road. Cross Moots Creek. The road becomes Springboro Road. Cross Indiana 18, then turn

(R) east on Chalmers Road

(L) north on Freeman Road. Jog right, then left again. Freeman Road becomes Highway 39/421 to Monticello. Go

(R) east on Beach Road to a beach, picnicking, and swimming. Follow Beach Road to its end. Retrace steps; follow Beach to

(L) south on North Illinois Street

(L) east on Washington, across Tippecanoe River. Stay on Washington and veer away from U.S. 24. Go past cemetery. Road curves right and becomes Riverview. Turn

(R) west on county road 100. Very soon after, turn

(L) south on 1125

(L) east on 1100

(R) south on 1050 into Yeoman. Road curves through Yeoman. Find your way to the elementary school and head east out of town on 975, to

(R) south and east onto 550

(R) south on 900. Cross Indiana 18 and turn

(R) west on Bicycle Bridge Road

(L) south on 1200, which becomes Grant Road as you leave White County and enter Tippecanoe County. Turn

(R) west, then south on 950

(R) west on Pretty Prairie Road across Tippecanoe River, past Lafayette Country Club, through town where it becomes Main Street. Cross railroad tracks

(L) south onto Railroad Avenue to the Tippecanoe Battlefield.

Dog-Day Morning
Bass Lake

Location:	In Indiana, 70 miles southeast of Chicago
Distance:	52 miles
Traffic:	Mostly light
Camping:	Tents and trailers at Bass Lake and Tippecanoe River state parks
Difficulty:	Moderate
Riding time:	6–7 hours
Directions:	Take I-65 south from Gary, then Indiana 10 east to Bass Lake.

The four corners linked by this route include a spit-and-polish military academy, a state park along seven miles of the Tippecanoe River, a drowsing farm community, and Indiana's fourth largest natural lake.

Bass Lake, whose Indian name *Winchetonqua* means "beautiful water," was first developed as a resort area for people from northern Indiana and Chicago, and many of its

gabled old homes date from the era when the Erie and
Nickel Plate railroads brought well-to-do vacationers here. It
wasn't until 1931 that the state moved to set aside some of
the lakeshore for the public. The result is skimpy, but all the
more to be valued—perhaps there might be nothing at all!
There's a thin strip of beach and a bathhouse, but parking
lots predominate. More than half the lake is under seven feet
deep.

In warm weather, just at sunup, a low, bright, motionless
mist may hang over much of this area, amplifying both si-
lence and distance so that you feel as if you're gliding
through a mirage.

Along the Tippecanoe the forest is thick and dark, en-
croaching on fields that are fallow or abandoned. Parks are
preserves where nature is kept beyond the reach of tractors
and discs, but how soon the forest moves forward again
when human influence recedes. Maybe it's the cultivated
land that is really the preserve.

A special area has been set aside at the Tippecanoe park
to observe white-tailed deer browsing during the morning
and evening. The water and woods attract many species of
birds too, some of them almost tropical-looking, others more
familiar but not often seen so closely, such as gray owls.

Culver has a distinct air that a visitor senses soon after
arriving, separating it from the run of towns its size in the
rural Midwest: a wider variety of restaurants (a cut above
the fast-food factories), sprucey clothing stores, and sports
cars. That's the rustle of out-of-town money you hear.

Lake Maxinkuckee is said to be one of the state's most
beautiful, and a lakeshore "cottage" may sell at $110,000.
Then there's Culver Military Academy, resplendent with
ivy, bricks, rolling lawns, and uniformed students. You may
see its scale-model, three-masted square-rigger or the sixty-
foot-model naval destroyer out on the lake or hear the happy
dissonance of chanting twelve-year-olds marching off to din-
ner in ragged formation.

The academy is a beauty, not just another campus. On summer Sundays there are class parades at 6:30 P.M. (12:30 P.M. in spring and fall).

Culver's opposite number, and a favorite hamlet of ours, is Monterey, a few miles south. It's the quintessential Midwest, with train tracks through town, a single traffic light, a looming grain elevator on the west end that you can see from four miles off as you approach on your bike, and a serene little riverside park with old-fashioned swings and a white belvedere made of crisscrossed laths. The whole place seems lightly dusted with corn pollen and laid aside from the mercantile tides that change things quickly and loudly. Nothing here louder than the buzzing bugs, and the long stretch from planting season through Indian summer is all dog days.

That expression has another meaning here, though: we counted fourteen dogs—loose, barking, and in hot pursuit— on the early morning when we took this ride. We've written elsewhere in this book about how to handle dogs, and they're certainly to be reckoned with here. Indiana's dogs are the most—er—challenging of all, though we weren't (and never have been) bitten.

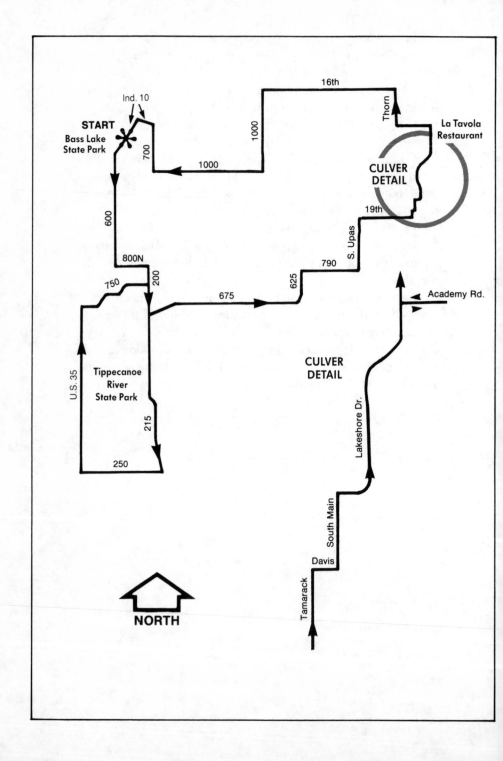

Dog-Day Morning

Start from the entrance to Bass Lake State Park, then go

(L) west on Indiana 10

(L) south on county road 600 across 800S and railroad tracks

(L) east on 800N

(R) south on 200, which becomes 215. Pass Haschell Bridge (public access to river), then

(R) west at 250 and across bridge

(R) north on U.S. 35. The park entrance is on the right. After leaving the park continue north on 35 to

(R) east at sign for Rising Sun Campground (road then turns north)

(R) east on 750

(R) south on 200

(L) east on 675 to Monterey, where the road becomes 700

(L) north at blinking red light in Monterey and pass Kleckner Park. The road becomes 625. Then turn

(R) east on 790, which becomes 900

(L) north on South Upas Road

(R) east on West 19th, across Indiana 17. The road curves left; go straight at the cemetery. The road becomes Tamarack Road. Jog right at Davis Street, then

(L) north on South Main

(R) east on Lakeshore Drive, curves north past city beach

(R) east at Academy Road to Culver Academy, then double back to

(R) north on Lakeshore Drive, across Highway 10/17

(L) west at La Tavola Restaurant

(R) north on Thorn Road

(L) west on 16th

(L) south on 1000 across Indiana 10, where the road curves to the right

(R) north on 700

(L) west on Indiana 10 to Bass Lake State Park.

Highballing at the Hesston steam museum

Rolling Prairie
Hesston

Location:	In Indiana, just below the Michigan border, 65 miles east of Chicago
Distance:	40 miles round trip
Traffic:	Light
Camping:	None
Difficulty:	A somewhat strenuous ride with many medium-sized hills
Riding time:	6–8 hours
Directions:	Take I-94 east to the first Michigan off-ramp onto U.S. 35 south; turn left at signs for Hesston just after re-entering Indiana, at county road 1000.

Rolling Prairie, Indiana 46371. Population: 500. Sounds like a great place to hide out from the underworld, doesn't it? Or from the FBI, depending on your daydreams. Who'd ever think of looking for you there, sitting on the porch of a frame house, reading the paper?

Rolling Prairie is a good place for cyclists who are taking it on the lam too, and looking for some shade and a soda.

This ride includes curiosities as well as beautiful prairie country. The Banholzer Winery displays the first vintage of champagne in the state, now selling for $125 a bottle. West of Hesston, where the ride begins, is the LaPorte County Historical Steam Society's 155-acre museum park. On summer weekends a half-dozen miniature and full-sized steam locomotives haul visitors around the society's trackage, and steam and antique buffs from three states meet here. There is a charge for the rides, but admission to the park is free.

The park also sports a working steam sawmill and a collection of steam tractors that expands and contracts, depending on what the society's members and others bring in for the weekend shows. The big event is on Labor Day weekend when, it is said, 20,000 people turn out.

On other weekends things can be slow, and visitors can take an unhurried look, if they wish, at an odd variety of boilers, pipes, throw rods, drive wheels, valves, and gauges. They all look purposeful and venerable but disconnected, at least for the time being, from any discernible function. A barn-sized shed shelters a conventional fire truck, the remains of a musical instrument on wheels, several tractors, and an assortment of unexplained gadgetry laid away here with intense fondness, pending later attention. The museum was a pet project of the late Elliot Donnelley of Chicago, of the publishing firm of the same name.

This is "raspberry country," if there is such a thing. In season (late June and July) you'll see signs for them on back-country phone poles and children patiently tending small tables with their pickings on sale at a dollar a box.

There is public access at Hudson Lake, which you'll see if you turn right at Chicago Road. On summer weekends it looks as though most of the population of upper LaPorte County have gathered to dip their toes at this small shoreline.

Hudson Lake was once a stop on the Great Sauk Indian Trail, which Sauk and Fox used to travel from what is now Detroit to what is now Chicago, and on to the lands of the Miami and the Illinois. It was also a "highway" for Iroquois from New York who came to do battle with the Chicago-area tribes.

Bendix Woods County Park, farther along and across Indiana 2 and U.S. 20, is the old Studebaker car corporation's proving grounds. The park's main offices, a museum, and a bookstore are housed in the Studebaker mansion, but the chief relic is a half-mile-long plot of red and white pines that spell out the word *Studebaker* in 250-foot letters, meant to be seen from the air. The living sign was a salute to the aviation industry when planted in 1936, and it is still a landmark for pilots as well as shade for picnickers.

The Studebaker Corporation preserved one of the few stands of beech and maple trees remaining in the area and reforested the rest of this 840-acre tract after purchasing it in 1926. A hike on one of the park trails will likely pass by the spectral remains of elm trees, killed by Dutch elm disease but still erect.

Out-of-county and out-of-state residents are required to pay a modest entrance fee. Useful brochures are available at the headquarters.

On the long leg of the trip from Bendix Woods to Rolling Prairie and then back to the steam museum, the forest is sometimes so lush that it arches completely over the road, and you'll feel as if you're riding through a tunnel. You need to get out of the Indiana sun for a while anyway, and no air-conditioned hamburger den is handy.

It's a long way between hamburgers in this part of the country. And that, maybe, is why you came to Rolling Prairie, isn't it? You're on the lam from all that.

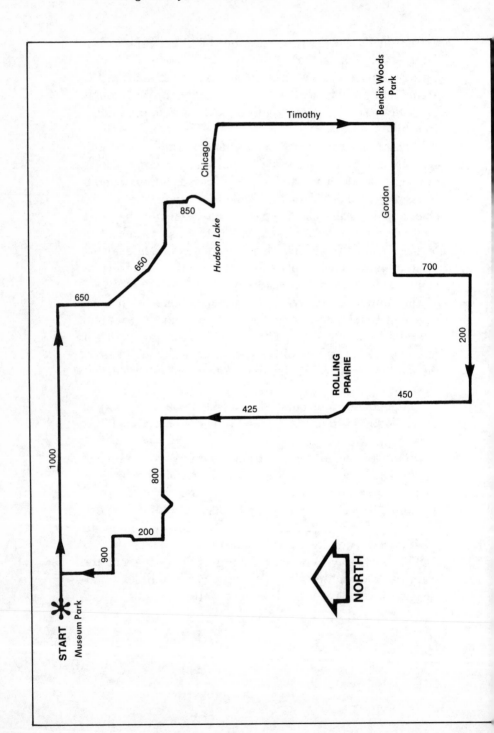

Rolling Prairie

Start at the LaPorte County Historical Steam Society museum park, and go

(L) east on county road 1000, through Hesston, past Banholzer Winery

(R) south on 650, which curves east

(R) south on 850 to Hudson Lake, right on Chicago Road to lake, or

(L) east on Chicago Road to

(R) south on Timothy Road through outskirts of New Carlisle, past U.S. 20 and Indiana 2, to Bendix Woods County Park (entrance on left). Continue south after park visit to

(R) west on Gordon Road

(L) south on 700, just before a church, through the "tunnel of trees" and past liquefied gas tanks to

(R) west on 200

(R) north on 450 across Indiana 2 and U.S. 20 and curve west into Rolling Prairie. The road becomes 425. Go on straight through town as the road curves north again. You'll see the St. Joseph Novitiate in the distance on your right, a mile and a half out this road. Go

(L) west on 800

(R) north on 200

(L) west on 900

(R) north at first paved road, and a brief

(L) west at 1000 takes you back to the museum park.

Dunestruck

Indiana Dunes

Location:	Around Lake Michigan, past Gary, Indiana, about 35 miles from Chicago
Distance:	23 miles round trip
Traffic:	Light
Camping:	In Indiana Dunes State Park, all types
Difficulty:	Easy
Riding time:	About 3 hours
Directions:	Take I-94 to the Indiana Dunes State Park, Indiana 49 exit. Follow signs for the state park. At U.S. 12 turn left. Follow 12 until its intersection with Mineral Springs Road. Turn right on Mineral Springs toward the railroad tracks. Park at the parking area and begin to ride northeast on the Calumet Trail.

Indiana Dunes National Lakeshore—8,000 acres of fine-grained sand, marshes, bogs, wetlands, and black oak and red pine forests, bordered by an industrial corridor whose 200 factories produce more than a thousand products.

This is a national park, decorated with slogans and slide shows quoting the national park values (preservation for future generations; respect for the land in its natural state), yet many say it's also a barrier to progress, keeping trade, production, and jobs from Indiana's small portion of lakeshore and hurting its already flagging economy.

Indiana Dunes has also become known as a bitter political battleground, picketed and petitioned by a group of lobbyists who've labored almost thirty years to keep the dunes a place apart. They are opposed by equally committed residents and legislators fighting for what they consider their economic life.

Out of this turmoil, Congress created the lakeshore park in 1966. It's a young park with some very raw edges but a beautiful and enlightening place for a bike ride.

The national lakeshore you see today is dotted with fences and private homes. Keep Out signs and Violators Will Be Towed warnings are more frequent than the tiny signs pointing the way to the public beach access. But it's here for the Chicagoans who ride the train to its beaches, the campers who sleep in its forests, the ecologists who study its bogs. Indiana Dunes is an urban park just beginning to come into its own.

The ride starts at the entrance to Dune Acres, a residential development. South of Dune Acres, toward West Beach, is the area that the Save the Dunes Council first formed to protect (it's not national park land—the council lost that first battle). Starting with just twenty members, the council made friends of conservationists and some politicians but also made enemies. Although they mounted impressive petition drives, their opposition was just as publicity-conscious. Some Indiana representatives even asked Congress to tear down Chicago's Loop and turn it into a national park, generously offering to donate the cattails and sand needed for the effort.

The first part of the trip is along the Calumet Trail, which Indiana calls its "first long-distance trail built exclusively for bicycling and hiking." Paralleling the Chicago, South Shore and South Bend Railroad, it runs in a straight line for 9.2 miles, ending at Mount Baldy in the national lakeshore park. As bicycle transportation, it's trafficless and quiet. But prepare yourself for some of the pitfalls—what the brochure calls hard-packed gravel but what is sometimes slow, loose, and slippery, and scenery that includes scrub vegetation and some enormous utility lines crackling overhead. (The trail runs through the property of the Northern Indiana Public Service Company.)

Although the trail is far from perfect, the National Park Service has plans for improving it. As it is now, there's only one sign on the trail pointing the way to the lakeshore. Plans for a number of secondary trails branching out from the Calumet Trail are in the works, according to park planner Stephen E. Whitesell. The park service is also planning to extend the trail both north and south to connect two metropolitan downtowns, Gary's and Michigan City's.

Consider following the trail's one sign to Indiana Dunes State Park. There are ten hiking trails, swimming, a wide beach, and concessions. It's apt to be jammed with people, but sometimes that's part of the fun.

The Calumet Trail ends at the 135-foot living sand dune, Mount Baldy. This entire dune moves as much as four feet per year. The catalysts are wind and water. There is a lack of vegetation to help keep the sand in one place. You can hike on this dune.

From here the ride takes you through a part of Beverly Shores, a residential area settled years ago by Lithuanians who found the area reminiscent of the Baltic Coast. In the 1920s a Chicago realtor built an impressive house with a private zoo high on one of the dunes and coaxed city dwellers out to his fledgling subdivision with rides on the Chicago, South Shore and South Bend Railroad.

These days the national park lures railroad patrons with "whistle-stop hikes" and shuttle buses that meet trains and take visitors to all park areas. The railroad does not presently carry bicycles, however, and there are no plans in the works to accommodate them, according to R. D. Bunton, passenger traffic manager for the railroad: "The cars weren't designed to transport bicycles, and there's a loading and unloading problem."

At Beverly Shores you'll ride past sweeping views of water and sand, as well as some expensive and unusual homes. When you feel like a dip, follow the wooden stairs down to the several beaches along this road.

After leaving the beach you'll find the visitor center, headquarters of the park's interpretive programs. Because there are a variety of environments here, southern and northern plants and animals exist side by side. It's not uncommon to discover northern birds like snow buntings chirping next to Louisiana water thrushes and Carolina wrens, or to spy southern dogwood plants growing near northern tundra bearberries and southwestern cactuses.

The park has also served as a laboratory for the "Father of Ecology," Henry Cowles. The scientist saw what is now called Cowles Bog by train on his way east. The area so fascinated him that he later returned to pioneer studies in plant succession at the bog and to teach at the University of Chicago.

The bogs themselves are both compelling and repelling. One of the early homesteaders described the environment as a place "which would have delighted the heart of a Borgia . . . where deadly nightshade and other horrid spotted plants, soaked in poisonous juices, grew and flourished amid venomous reptiles."

Although this account may have been an exaggeration (she probably meant the salamanders, lizards, and harmless but ugly hog-nosed snakes of the area), the bogs do support some treacherous plants, especially if you're an insect. One pitcher plant was discovered to have gorged itself to death on a half-digested tree frog. Three other varieties of carnivorous plants grow in the shady, swampy areas of the park, but they usually eat ants and flies, not frogs. The reason they crave meat is biological. The bog soil does not have enough nutrients to sustain the plants, so they must get their vitamins and minerals in other ways.

These bogs are not normally open to the public, but park rangers lead guided hikes through them from time to time. Rangers also lead "joggers' specials," runs along the beaches and trails of the park; a "wild edibles hike," where participants sample dandelion leaves and other delicacies; and a program called "Duneland Dimensions," which combines slides, color videotape, and original electronic music.

The Bailly Homestead is the site of the annual Dunes Folk Festival, sponsored by the National Park Service. Everything is traditional—the jaw harps, dulcimers, and folk guitars; the Swedish folk songs; the silversmithing and soap making, horseshoeing and trapping demonstrations; the roast pork, Indian fry bread, and apple cider. And it's free.

Bailly was a missionary and, at first, the only Catholic between Detroit and Fort Dearborn (now Chicago). During the festival a traditional religious service is re-created.

A short hike away is the Chelbourg farm. Settled by Swedes in 1863, the farm is being developed as a living history demonstration. Rangers dressed in traditional clothes demonstrate farm life, gardening, and cooking as it might have been during Chelbourg's time. One elaborate steel machine wove wire into a line of fence as we watched.

Although the riding time is relatively short, you can tell there's a lot to enjoy here. Pack a lunch, take a swim, and take your time.

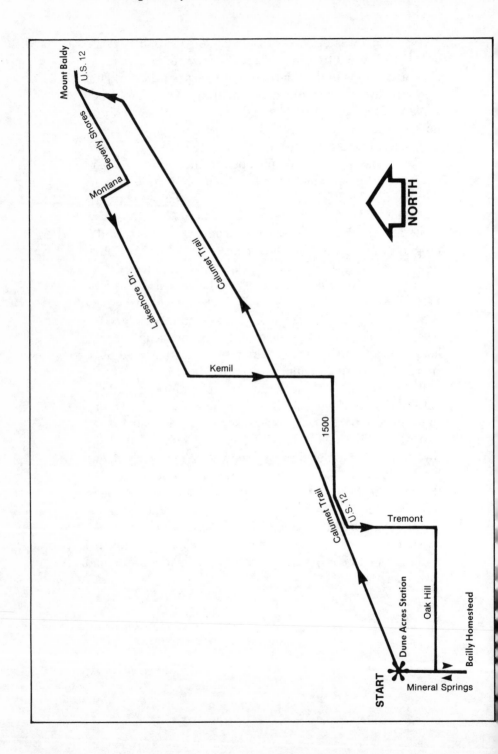

Dunestruck

Begin at the Dune Acres parking lot at the intersection of
Mineral Springs Road and the Calumet Trail. Proceed northeast on the trail. You can detour to the state park when you
see the small sign for the access path, just after the Indiana
49 overpass. When the trail runs out after 9.2 miles, cross the
bad gravel parking lot and go

(L) north on U.S. 12 to Mount Baldy turnoff (almost immediately). From Mount Baldy, retrace steps out from
parking area, then go

(R) west on Beverly Shores Drive. There is no street sign.
Then

(R) north on Montana Street

(L) west on Lakeshore Drive to the end of it

(L) south onto what becomes Kemil Road

(R) west at bike barn just before U.S. 20. There's no street
sign, but it's county road 1500. Then

(L) west on U.S. 12 for a short, busy stretch

(L) south on Tremont Road. Cross U.S. 20, then Indiana 49,
to

(R) west on East Oak Hill Road, at the church. Cross U.S.
20 again, then

(L) south on Mineral Springs Road to Bailly Homestead. Af-
ter a visit there, retrace steps along Mineral Springs
Road, cross Oak Hill Road and U.S. 12 to the Dune
Acres lot.

MICHIGAN

Woods, Wine, and Waves
Warren Dunes

Location: 65 miles northeast of Chicago, near the
                 town of Three Oaks, Michigan

Distance: 32 miles round trip

Traffic: Light; heavy on 1/4-mile stretch on Red
                 Arrow Highway

Camping: All varieties of camping at Warren
                 Dunes State Park

Difficulty: Easy to moderate

Riding time: About 4 hours

Directions: Take I-94 around Lake Michigan to the
                 U.S. 12 exit. Take U.S. 12 east to
                 Lakeside Road. Turn left on Lakeside,
                 then right on Warren Woods Road to
                 Warren Woods.

Where would you expect to find a quiet country winery
that grows all its own grapes, that wins wine awards, and
whose wine was even served at diplomatic dinners? France?
Germany? Or maybe even California?

169

Unlikely as it may seem, Michigan has a winery that fits this description. It's folded into rolling hills on a back road near the tiny town of Baroda. It makes an exceptionally pleasant stop on a thirty-two-mile loop through Berrien County that takes you from a "forest primeval" to the oceanlike shores of Lake Michigan.

Start your trip at the Forest Primeval sign at Warren Woods (it was probably dubbed this by someone who hiked into its dense greenery). A stream runs through the preserve, as do sinuous trails. There are no picnic facilities at the woods, though, or at the winery, so plan on eating farther along your ride at Baroda Community Park or at Warren Dunes State Park.

One of the virtues of this ride is the nature of the roads. Instead of flat, straight paths, the gently uplifted countryside offers hills to push up and coast down and some serpentine curves to roll around. The scenery is lush. A nursery grows acres of ornamentals from Christmas pines to juniper bushes.

And then there are the orchards. Apples, just beginning to plump out by mid-June, blueberries, and cherries. Michigan is one of the world's leading producers of blueberries and grows 70 percent of this country's tart red cherries.

As you approach the Tabor Hill Winery, at a short detour off Snow Road, a sign announces the operation with a large carving of Bacchus, god of wine.

The free tours of the winery are sometimes led by the owner, Leonard Olsen, or his daughter Julie. Olsen started commuting from Chicago's South Side on weekends to start his grapes in 1968. In 1970, as the first crop was maturing, the family moved to Michigan for keeps.

Although the ambience is casual, the business of wine making is not. Olsen has made trips to Europe, especially France and Germany, to study wine-making techniques. His latest project is a European ice-wine, made by picking grapes in 25° weather while they're still frozen.

The owners like to compare Tabor Hill to Europe. The

unpredictable climate, the rolling hills, and the sandy soil resemble European wine regions, they say.

So does the method of wine making. Unlike many larger wineries, every wine sold by Tabor Hill is made from grapes grown by them. Most of the grapes are picked by hand. Michigan-born President Ford honored the winery by serving Tabor Hill to the Austrian ambassador, making it the first midwestern wine to be served at the White House.

The first Sunday after Labor Day the winery holds a Harvest Festival. The grapes are blessed, then participants shed their shoes and crush the first batch the old-fashioned way, to the accompaniment of bluegrass and polka music. At one harvest festival, blonde-haired Julie got into a grape fight with friends and discovered the hard way that grape juice turns yellow hair blue.

After leaving Tabor Hill, the ride takes you through the town of Baroda. Look for the sign advertising Sherman's Ice Cream at the local drugstore. The ice cream is made with liberal chunks of fresh fruit and comes from Michigan. Or if health foods are more to your liking, sample local fruit at one of the roadside stands. Strawberries were in season when we rode, but the offerings change weekly.

If you want a picnic lunch, Baroda has a small, quiet town park with picnic tables. Look for it off to your left as you head out of town.

From here, the ride edges toward Lake Michigan. It's hard to see the lake, but the isolated sand dunes here and there and the light, dry soil are evidence of the changing topography.

Warren Dunes State Park makes a cool, relaxing stop, especially in the summer heat. Its large beach, towering sand dunes, and grassy picnic areas are breezier than inland spots, and numerous bathhouses make it easy to take a dip. Hiking trails intersect the dunes and woods too. The park is free for bicyclists, but cars are charged admission. There are full camping facilities also, but out-of-state campers must buy a permit.

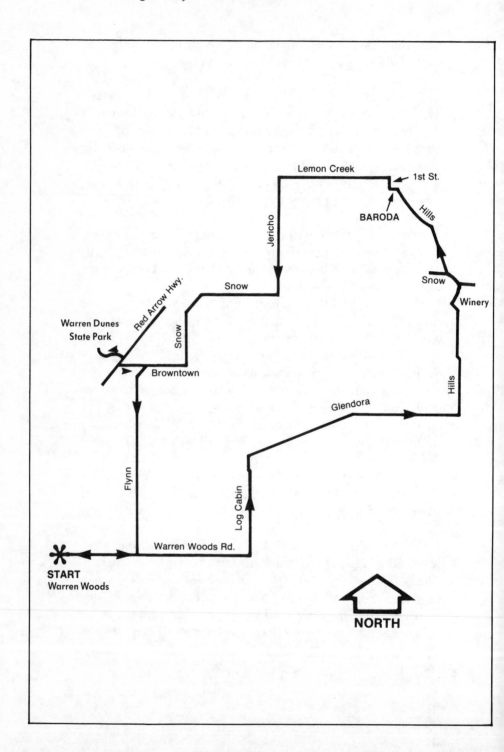

Woods, Wine, and Waves

Begin at the sign for Warren Woods, along Warren Woods Road. Go east on Warren Woods Road to Log Cabin Road, then

(L) north on Log Cabin Road

(R) east on Glendora Road

(L) north on Hills Road

(L) west on Snow Road to where it becomes Hills Road. Continue west and north on Hills Road to Baroda. Then

(R) north on 1st Street

(L) west on Lemon Creek Road in the center of town (a picnic area is on the left as you leave town)

(L) south on Jericho Road

(R) west and south on Snow Road

(R) west on Browntown Road

(R) north on Red Arrow Highway to Warren Dunes State Park

(R) south from Warren Dunes State Park

(L) east on Browntown Road

(R) south on Flynn Road

(R) west on Warren Woods Road to Warren Woods.

Drawbridge and "De Zwaan," on Windmill Island

Tiptoe Through the Tulips
Holland

Location: Van Buren State Park and north, about
                 100 miles northeast of Chicago along
                 Lake Michigan
Distance: Approximately 92 miles long
Traffic: Light to moderate, with some heavy
                 traffic in Holland
Camping: All varieties at Van Buren State Park
                 and Holland State Park
Difficulty: Easy but long—requires stamina
Riding time: 13–16 hours (a 2-day ride)
Directions: Take I-94 north toward South Haven,
                 Michigan. Exit before South Haven at
                 the signs for Van Buren State Park.

A tall, fat, powerful windmill making steady circles in the
sky; pink-cheeked, costumed girls on wooden shoes spinning
each other around in noisy dance patterns; and mailbox
names like Kraak, Plagamaars, Van Den Bosch, and Schaap.
Sound intriguing?

Holland, Michigan, and its sister city Zeeland are ideal for a weekend bicycle trip. Holland is large enough to have a comfortable complement of motels and restaurants and, if you are hardy, a state park campground.

The area has novelty. The attractions, though somewhat commercial, are varied and educational. People of the Netherlands did settle the cities, and the heritage is as deep-rooted as the acres of tulip gardens.

Included in this journey are several waterside parks, a winery, museums, the shores of Lake Michigan, a chain ferry, and, if you time it right, fresh apple cider and cider donuts or a taste of the world's largest blueberry muffin.

First Day

Your expedition begins at the 326-acre Van Buren State Park, with its wooded dunes. There are no hiking or naturalist activities here, but it's a fine place for a swim.

The trip takes you east into the rolling Michigan countryside. Civilization springs up in tenuous patches—a deserted church; a flashing red light next to a long-closed service station; the town of Pullman, where almost every building is abandoned. You'll pass through Breedsville, Grand Junction, Bravo, and Pearl—towns with proud, evocative names. They're so small you can't blink or you'll miss them, even on your bicycle!

Fennville seems almost metropolitan by comparison. On Saturdays its main street is jammed with farm families and migrant workers, all in for the week's shopping. There are many goodies for the road-weary bicyclist—bakery goods, ice cream, and, on the outskirts of town, fresh fruit from local farms. Apples, blueberries, cherries, and even grapes grow around here. Some of the farms are U-Pick.

A short detour leads to Crane Orchards, 1½ miles from town. They sell home-pressed apple ciders, blends of different varieties like Ida Reds and Jonathans. You can have lunch and fruit-filled baked goods there too.

Just past Lake Hutchins on a county road is the Fenn Valley Winery. Besides tasting wine, you can observe the wine-making process at your own pace from galleries above the plant.

Even though you don't travel along Lake Michigan this first day, the stretch has some lovely stops by the water. A fishing access area on the wide, placid Kalamazoo River is especially scenic because the river curves around on itself, and cars have to cross it slowly over a one-lane wooden bridge. There's also a small, lily-padded lake called Baseline.

Maybe it's only psychological, but the countryside seems to flatten out at the approach to Zeeland. The Dutch immigrants who sailed to America in 1847 chose this area for its terrain; the flat, fertile land and sand dunes reminded them of home.

The 457 settlers seeking religious freedom produced a sizable community. Zeeland's population of 5,000, added to Holland's nearly 30,000 residents, may be the reason the cities call themselves "the center of Dutch culture in the United States."

Zeeland has a thriving downtown, partly because it is not competing with a shopping mall. And a bicycle-route system connects some of the less-traveled thoroughfares.

If you're interested in local history, detour a few blocks east of your ride, in the opposite direction down Central (see the map). The first block of the detour, at 50 West Central, has the oldest house in town after the era of wooden shacks and log cabins. Built in 1849, it stood three blocks west until 1900, when it was placed on rollers and moved to its present site. This location was then regarded as a lonely spot on a muddy buggy path, far out of town.

On this same block, at Central and Church streets, is the site of the Zeelanders' second log church, built in 1849. The first church was too small for the dramatic influx of immigrants. The half-acre lot cost ninety cents then.

At 120 South Church is the 1872 Victorian and Gothic home of Zeeland's first physician and village president.

When he died, the house was believed to be haunted, and it stood empty for twelve years.

The house at 320 East Central was the home of the wealthy Baron Daniel Van Sytzama. Look for the small touches on the Greek Revival mansion, like the stained, leaded, beveled, and etched window glass. Retrace your route, then proceed through Zeeland and on to Holland.

The city of Holland will require careful riding. There are some trafficky patches, but bicycles are common enough in town. Your route takes you by a wooden-shoe factory, where you can put a quarter in the turnstile and watch factory workers demonstrate their art in three ways: entirely by hand, with a bygone method using antique machinery, and with a more modern "dual action" method that copies the form of one shoe into another block of poplar or aspen. You may even see Fred Oldemulders, who at eighty still carves shoes as he learned to at age fifteen in the Netherlands. Fred has carved over 300,000 "klompen" in his career.

Another stop is Windmill Island. It's a municipal park with a two-dollar admission, but its managers seem to be keeping it free of tacky commercialism. Its most striking feature is De Zwaan, the 200-year-old windmill imported from Holland. This was the last windmill the government allowed to leave Holland. It stands as high as a twelve-story building and is the only Dutch windmill operating in the United States. You can buy the flour that it grinds. There are also Dutch dances, an ornate carousel for kids, a movie on Holland, and a drawbridge.

Near Windmill Island is the Baker Furniture Museum. Although there is a small separate admission, the museum has some unusual features, including a chair hall with a cross section of 100 chairs, from antique to modern.

One block off our route is the Netherlands Museum with two authentic Dutch rooms and a 100-year-old dollhouse. You can extend your tour of Holland to include its other attractions: the Poll Museum of Transportation, Veldheer's

Tulip Gardens, the Dutch Village, and another wooden-shoe factory. Or you might be more than ready for a motel and a hot bath. This first stretch of ride totals forty-five miles. If you're energetic, Holland has a summer theater too. One summer this group presented plays ranging from the musical *George M* to the comedy *The Amorous Flea*.

If you want to camp in Holland, locate a city map and ride around Lake Macatawa to Holland State Park. You will probably encounter heavy traffic en route to the park. But there is camping and 2,200 feet of beach to enjoy when you arrive.

Second Day

The following morning, ride out of Holland toward Saugatuck. A town of 1,000 that swells to many times its size each summer, Saugatuck is now becoming as well known for its vacation attractions as it used to be for its art colony. One remnant of the art colony is the Valleau Studio, which sells replicas of ornamental brass sand-castings made by colonial methods.

Galleries and unusual shops are here, as are dozens of picturesque vistas—jumbles of ships in the harbor; a yacht moving lazily beside the long wooden pier; tiny, tempting restaurants with bay views built almost in the water.

Its history is a strong part of the village. Saugatuck was constructed near the buried city of Singapore, Michigan, which was founded as a boom town to rival Chicago. Singapore was built near an ancient Indian burial ground. Learn more of the facts at the historical museum, as well as the history of lumbering and shipbuilding in the area.

There are plenty of other things to do here. The town claims the only hand-operated chain ferry in the country, a replica of the boat that carried early settlers and their supplies across the Kalamazoo beginning in 1838. For fifty cents you can ride to the Douglas side, pulled by a 380-foot-long,

200-pound chain connected to each bank of the river.

That's not the only boat. The S.S. *Keewatin*, moored in Douglas, is a Great Lakes coal-burning, hand-fired, overnight-passenger steamer once owned by the Canadian Pacific Railroad. In its heyday it could accommodate 288 passengers and 86 crewmembers. Now it's a maritime museum. An old stern-wheeler, *Queen of the Saugatuck*, and a sixty-foot cruise ship are other nautical ways to view the area. You can rent a canoe or paddle boat on the Kalamazoo River or sail over the dunes on a dune schooner. There's a Gilbert and Sullivan Festival in summer and a lighted boat parade during the Venetian Festival in July.

Leaving the community, you'll ride south along Lake Michigan past some sizable lakefront homes and even more sizable lakefront views. There is a county park and beach to break up the pedaling as you return via the outskirts of South Haven. The city is known for its annual Blueberry Festival, where residents enter and sell their blueberry pies and homemade blueberry ice cream. You can tour surrounding blueberry farms or just gape at the world's largest blueberry muffin. The festival is usually in July.

From South Haven, the ride returns to Van Buren State Park.

Tiptoe Through the Tulips

Start at Van Buren State Park. Go out the main park road (Ruggles Road), then

(R) south on Blue Star Highway a short distance

(L) east on CR 380

(L) north at the blinking red light in Breedsville

(L) west at CR 384 a short distance

(R) north just before the railroad tracks

(L) west at the post office in the village of Grand Junction

(R) north just after Grand Junction on CR 215. The road curves to the left. Then

(L) west on Baseline Road. Follow it for .2 mile on gravel for a view of Baseline Lake. Go

(R) north on 56th Street. The road jogs to the right as it crosses the Chesapeake and Ohio Railroad tracks. Continue north through Pullman, Bravo, and Pearl. Go

(L) west at the sign for Fennville, and soon after

(R) north on 57th Street into Fennville. Refreshments and restaurants are here.

Or detour

(L) west on Michigan 89 to Cider Farms (1½ miles from Fennville) or

(L) west on Michigan 89 to

(L) south on 58th

(R) west at third intersection around Hutchins Lake and west to Fenn Valley Winery. Return to Fennville. From Fennville, go

(L) north on first paved road (56th Street)

(L) west on 128th a short distance to

(R) north on 56th Street a short distance,

(L) west and north on 130th Street, which curves 90° to the right and goes over a one-lane wooden bridge across the Kalamazoo River. Follow it as it curves left (west) under the train tracks, with a river access on the left. Then

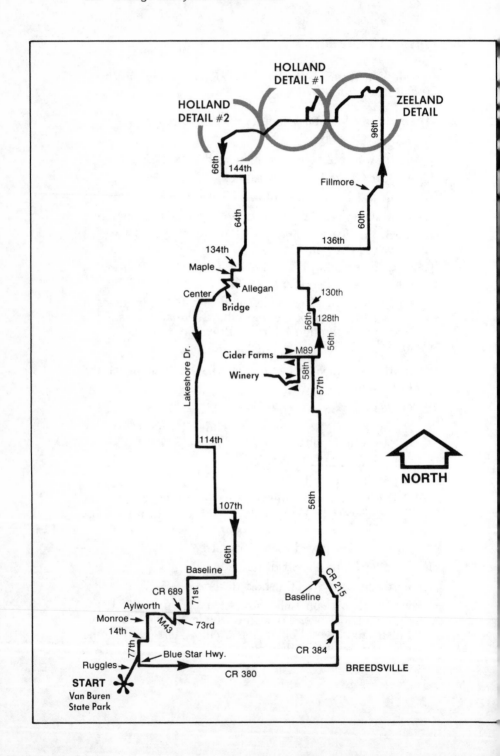

(R) north at the first paved road

(R) east on 136th Avenue

(L) north on 60th Street

(R) east and north on Fillmore Road. Road turns due east again. Go

(L) north at sign for Zeeland. The road becomes 96th into Zeeland. Refreshments and shops are here. Then

(L) west on Central.

Or **detour**

(R) east on Central to historic homes (see text). Then west on Central to

(L) south on Taft

(R) west on Huizenga

(R) north on 104th

(L) southwest on Paw Paw Drive. Paw Paw turns south and west again, and goes into Holland. Turn

(L) south on Hope Avenue

(R) west on 16th Street. The wooden-shoe factory is here. Continue on 16th to

(R) north on College

(R) east on 6th Street

(L) north on the Windmill Island entrance road. Windmill Island is here. Retrace path back to 6th and south on College.

Or **detour**

(R) west one block on 12th Street to see Netherlands Museum. Return to College, ride south to

(R) west on 16th Street

(L) southwest then west on South Shore Drive

(L) south on Jenson. Jog

(R) west on 32nd, and immediately

(L) south on 66th

(L) east on 144th

(R) south on 64th to the Blue Star Highway

(R) west and then immediately

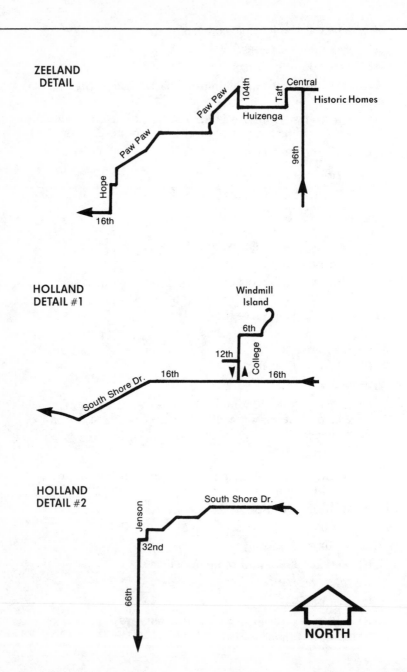

ZEELAND
DETAIL

Central
Historic Homes
104th
Taft
Huizenga
Paw Paw
Paw Paw
96th
Hope
16th

HOLLAND
DETAIL #1

Windmill
Island
6th
12th
College
South Shore Dr.   16th
16th

HOLLAND
DETAIL #2

Jenson
South Shore Dr.
32nd
66th

NORTH

(L) south on 64th again, which jogs again on 136th Avenue and continues south, to

(R) west on 134th across the Blue Star Highway

(L) south on Maple, which is dirt for .3 mile

(R) west onto Allegan Street into Saugatuck. Historical museum is here. You can turn right at the museum to city shops, marina, and restaurants. Retrace steps past museum to

(R) west over the bridge on the Blue Star Highway. Veer

(R) west onto Center Street toward lake. From here you can turn off to Oval Beach and the Douglas attractions (see text). Then

(L) south on Lakeshore Drive until it merges with the Blue Star Highway. Almost immediately turn

(L) east onto 114th Avenue

(R) south at the first intersection after the overpass

(L) east at the Casco Town Hall (107th Avenue)

(R) south on 66th Street

(R) west on Baseline Road

(L) south on 71st Street across the Black River

(R) west on CR 689. Keep going straight when 689 veers left. Go

(L) south on 73rd Street

(R) northwest on Michigan 43, over the expressway and across the Blue Star Highway

(L) west onto Aylworth Avenue

(L) south on Monroe Boulevard, which merges into the Blue Star Highway

(R) west on 14th Avenue

(L) south on 77th Street. Jog onto the Blue Star Highway for a few yards, then

(R) south onto Ruggles Road, and back to Van Buren State Park.

Paw Paw pastoral with bicycle

Fruit Loop
Paw Paw

Location:	Michigan, about 100 miles east and north of Chicago
Distance:	22 miles
Traffic:	Mostly light, one short stretch excepted
Camping:	Some private campgrounds in the area
Difficulty:	A breeze, except for a mile of gravel road
Riding time:	3–5 hours
Directions:	Take I-94 to Exit 60 and begin your ride at the city park in Paw Paw.

This ride is at the geographical limit of the range of this book but within the physical limits of most beginning bike riders, with gently rolling hills that seem to rise under your handlebars just long enough to make the coast back down the other side seem welcome.

In spring you can see what look like puny green strings of peas forming on the hundreds of acres of vineyards along this route; as time passes, they swell into voluptuous bunches of grapes, which supply the several wineries nearby. You'll also see cherries and blueberries, and fruit stands selling all these as well as melons and apples.

We'd tip you off to the best vintages to try at the three wineries along this route, but we're untutored in the subtleties. On the other hand, we know what we like: each winery has free wine tasting. You can decide what's good for yourself. Just don't absorb too much of this local color if you have a lot of pedaling ahead of you, especially on a hot day.

The Vendramino Winery may be the smallest open-to-the-public winery in Michigan. Owner Robert Coleman explains, "My girlfriend's grandfather's name is Vendramino, so we called it that. You can't call a winery the Coleman Winery, can you?" He is the inventor of a redolent onion cooking wine.

When we set off on our ride, long, heavy gusts of wind roared in the trees and seemed to flatten our ears against our heads. It never did subside, but within the first mile or so we began to enjoy its presence and dropped down into a lower gear range to pull through it.

Playing out in the wind is something most people have to give up about the time they leave elementary school. Like hills, wind seems to be an adversity, something to fight against. But it isn't long before cyclists begin to look forward to both as a needed change. Riding into the teeth of a full wind that is pushing cloud shadows over the fields is to be savored.

Paw Paw is named after a fairly common midwestern tree that bears decorous flowers and small, banana-shaped fruit. Its botanical name is *Asimina triloba*, but why name a town that? The town is at the east end of the loop, and the Lake Cora Golf Club, which has a couple of picnic tables under the trees, is at the western end. At Lake Cora is a small, grassy public access area for a cool soak on a hot ride, just down the road from the Vendramino establishment. Unfortunately, there's no way to get from the golf club to those two places without traveling about a mile on the Red Arrow Highway. This thoroughfare has everything: consistently heavy traffic; deep, soft gravel shoulders impossible to ride on; crumbling asphalt at its edges; and, finally, two quite narrow lanes.

We've provided a quiet alternative route that avoids all this, but then you miss Lake Cora and the little winery too. If you want to see them, watch the traffic for a minute or two on the Red Arrow Highway. If it's light, ride the half-mile to the turnoff. If it's heavy, walk your bike to the turnoff along the gravel shoulder—it won't take long.

In late June you can stop and pick strawberries at a big patch just before Three Mile Lake, if you like. Light, moist fruit is good to bring on a bike ride no matter where you buy it. The road around the lake, by the way, is hard-packed dirt and gravel, bumpy but not impossible to negotiate, and it's only a mile long.

Plan to spend some time at the park in Paw Paw. There's a wooden footbridge out to an island in the lake and several nice spots to picnic. Another section of the park and the lake is almost hidden on the south side of Michigan Street.

START
City Park

PAW PAW
DETAIL

35½

53rd

52nd

Hazen

Ackley Lake

Michigan

Grempe

Commercial

Paw Paw Rd.

52nd

PAW PAW
DETAIL

41st

56th

42nd

671

Red Arrow Hwy.

671

Lake Cora

Paw Paw Rd.

NORTH

Fruit Loop

Start at the Paw Paw city park's east side picnic grounds and parking lot. Look for the old brick power plant at the north end of the lake and head west on the little road that passes in front of the plant. Then go

(L) south on 35½

(R) west on 53rd

(L) south on Hazen

(R) west on 52nd

(L) south on 41st

(R) west on 56th

(L) south on county road 671 to the golf club. If you don't wish to visit Lake Cora and the Vendramino Winery, return to 56th, turn east (right), and skip the next seven steps. Otherwise, continue south on 671 after the golf club and turn

  (L) east on Red Arrow Highway

  (R) south on 671

  (R) west at the small sign that says Lake Cora, just before the expressway overpass; retrace steps back to

  (L) north on 671

  (R) east on Red Arrow Highway

  (L) north on 42nd

  (R) east on 56th

(R) south on 41st and cross the highway. A gravel road begins after a mile; follow it around Three Mile Lake, to

(L) south, then east on Paw Paw Road

(R) east on Michigan

(R) south on Grempe

(L) east on Commercial to wineries; retrace steps to

(L) west on Michigan

(R) north on Hazen

(R) east on 53rd

(L) north on 35½

(R) east on power plant road to Start.

WISCONSIN

Yerkes Observatory: cosmic rococo

As You Lake It
Geneva

Location:	Southern Wisconsin, around Lake Geneva, about 85 miles from Chicago
Distance:	45 miles, plus a 12-mile optional loop
Traffic:	Mostly light; some heavy sections
Camping:	Car and walk-in at Bigfoot Beach State Park
Difficulty:	Fairly difficult; long, with some tough hills
Riding time:	7–10 hours
Directions:	Turn off Illinois 53 onto U.S. 14 at Arlington Heights and follow U.S. 14 to Walworth, Wisconsin.

Lake Geneva's long shoreline is dotted with resorts, tourist attractions, vacation-home developments, and weekend getaway destinations, including a Playboy Club. As always, these mean a tide of auto traffic that does not bode well for bikers.

The route suggested here circumnavigates the lake but only touches it twice, and you'll miss most of the traffic as a result. The back country of southern Wisconsin is a congenial buffer zone to pedal around in by day. After sundown you can don your party clothes—the ones you've kept neatly folded in your knapsack—and go nightclubbing at the shore.

The first lakeshore stop on this ride is on an optional loop to Bigfoot Beach State Park. If you're bike camping, the fee is much less than if you bring your car. The camping area is on one side of the road and the beach is on the other side.

It may be called Bigfoot Beach, but if your feet are bigger than size nine, they won't fit on this strand without getting your toes wet. The narrow beach is really cramped by the busy highway behind it.

Much farther along, the route brings you to the western shore of the lake at a marina development called Fontana Village. Here you can seek out a little park at the curve of Kinzie Avenue. If you pass between two brick pillars after reading a plaque about the Indians, there's a pathway along the lake to the left, which leads to a larger park. It's easy to see why this beautiful lake has attracted so many vacationers for so many years.

A fascinating stop is the Yerkes Astronomical Observatory of the University of Chicago. Tours are given at half-hour intervals, and there is no admission charge. Tour groups are told something of the history of the observatory and taken up to the home dome of what is referred to as the Great Refractor, a twenty-ton, sixty-three-foot tube housing a forty-inch lens, the largest ever made and successfully used in a telescope.

Graduate students stand under the telescope, give a short briefing, and answer questions, but the dome is so huge that questions and answers are frequently lost in echoes.

There's a great temptation in the air to somehow sneak over and peek into the telescope while everyone is discussing it. It is so powerful that it can resolve an image the size of a quarter at a distance of 1,000 miles.

Alas, the place is open to the public for a scant ninety minutes to two hours a week, because it is a working scientific laboratory, research station, and library. The hours are 1:30 to 3:00 P.M. on Saturdays, June through September, and 10 A.M. to 12:00 noon on Saturdays the rest of the year. It may be hard to hit at the right time if you're biking. If you're uncertain, either begin your ride here and return early or finish somewhere else early enough to return in the car.

The outside of the observatory is also splendid. At the rear entrance, for example, there are some ornate and decidedly unscientific-looking columns, full of cosmic esoterica that look as if they were copied from Merlin the Magician's wizard hat.

There's a story behind at least one of these curiosities, passed down among astronomy students over the nine decades since the observatory was built. A face with a very long nose appears several times on one column. Above the tip of the nose is a rough patch in the otherwise smooth image.

It is said that the face is that of Charles T. Yerkes, the Chicago businessman who financed the observatory in 1892. When it was under construction, legend has it, there was also a bee next to Yerkes's swollen nose, representing University of Chicago President William Rainey Harper, who had "stung" Yerkes for the $500,000 gift used to build the observatory. When Harper visited the construction site and divined the message in the masonry, he ordered the bee chipped away—hence the rough spot.

An ironic twist in the legend is that Yerkes did not really have the money he pledged. He was in some financial difficulty at the time. But when word got out of his immense gift to the university, his credit rating shot skyward and he was able to borrow enough money to stay afloat and make new investments. These later yielded more than enough money to pay off his pledge—or so the tale goes.

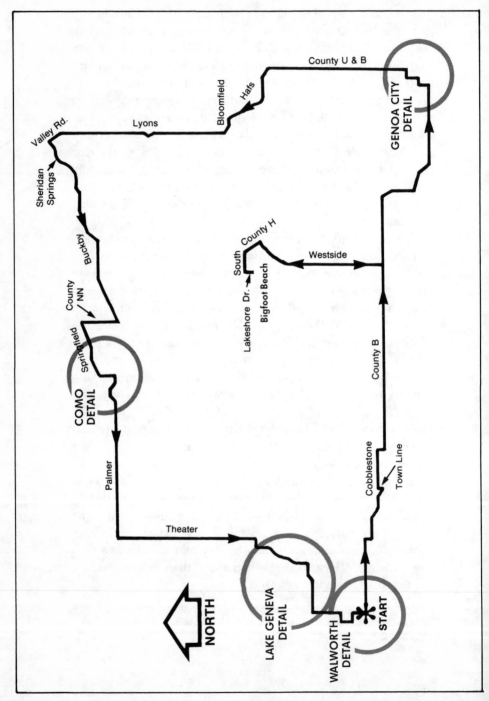

As You Lake It

Begin at the corner of Devil's Lane and Main Street (U.S. 14) just south of the town square in Walworth, Wisconsin. Go east on Devil's Lane, past Bigfoot High School. Turn

(R) south where the road ends, onto an unmarked road. Cross railroad tracks. The road curves left, then right, then right again, then left. Jog

(L) north on Town Line Road. Cross the railroad tracks, then

(R) east on Cobblestone Road, which becomes County Trunk B. Cross Wisconsin 120. If you're going to Bigfoot Beach, turn

   (L) north on Westside Road

   (L) northwest on County Trunk H

   (L) west on South Street

   (L) south on Lakeshore Drive to Bigfoot Beach. Retrace path to County Trunk B. Proceed east on County Trunk B to Genoa City. Then

(L) north on Freeman

(R) east on Walworth

(L) north on Sumner

(R) east on Franklin

(L) north on County Trunks U and B (all one road)

(L) west, then north on Hafs Road

(L) west on Bloomfield Road

(R) north on Lyons Road

(L) west on Valley Road just outside the village of Lyons

(L) southwest on Sheridan Springs

(R) west on Buckby as Sheridan Springs curves. Cross Wisconsin 36 and pass the Mount Fuji Ski Area. Then

(R) north on County NN

(L) west on Springfield Road

(R) west on a paved road at a mailbox that says The Patnaudes. Jog

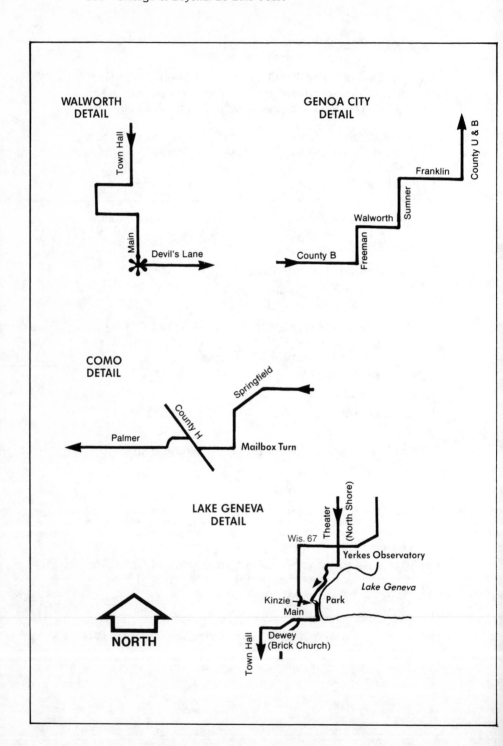

(R) west on County Trunk H. Almost immediately, take the first left at the Y in the road and go

(R) west on Palmer Road and across Wisconsin 67

(L) south on Theater Road and across Wisconsin 50

(L) east on Wisconsin 67 to Yerkes Observatory (use bordering street on the north side), then retrace your steps to Theater Road. Go

(L) south on Theater Road, which becomes North Shore Road as it curves around Lake Geneva

(L) on Kinzie Road to Fontana Village on the lake. Watch for vest-pocket park and path on your left, with bench and pillars. Part of the village is closed to cars, but ride along the marina to

(R) west at The Wharf, Limited, on Main Street. Cross Wisconsin 67. The road curves left. Turn

(R) west on Dewey Street, which becomes Brick Church Road

(L) south on Town Hall Road into Walworth. Go around the square to your right. Turn

(R) south on Main Street to Start.

Seventy-Sixer
Milwaukee

Location:	The city and county of Milwaukee, about 80 miles from Chicago
Distance:	76 miles round trip
Traffic:	Ranges from nonexistent on separate bike trails, to light on parkway roads, to moderate and occasionally heavy on city streets
Camping:	None near the ride; closest is the southern unit of Kettle Moraine State Forest, southwest of Waukesha, near Eagle
Difficulty:	Difficult because of length and occasional heavy traffic
Riding time:	11 hours
Directions:	Take I-94 north toward Milwaukee. Get off at the Rawson Avenue exit, south of the city. Go left on Rawson, left on South 27th and left on Drexel. You can park by the side of the road or at the park a little farther along this block.

It's hard to think of bustling, built-up, industrial Milwaukee, nicknamed "the machine shop of America," as a pleasant place for a bike ride. This urban center for five counties, with $6 billion per year in industrial output, is regarded as one of the country's most blue-collar cities. And the products are as brawny and machinelike as you can get. Milwaukee produces more diesel and gasoline engines, outboard motors, motorcycles, tractors, wheelbarrows, and padlocks than any other place in the world. What did we leave out? You'll guess it by the smell of malt in the air: beer.

With all this heavyweight production and factory hustle, it seems as if the likes of a ten-speed would be a little outdistanced. But thanks to the efforts of a group of enthusiastic bicyclists and the Milwaukee County Parks Commission, there is a seventy-six-mile loop around and through Milwaukee that skirts most of the congestion and shows you the greener, more restful side of the city.

The loop was a project for the Bicentennial, and that's also the reason for its seventy-six-mile length. Twenty-four of these miles are off the road, twenty-three miles are on parkway drives, and twenty-nine are on city streets. That's a pretty good ratio when you consider the 685,000 people in the city proper.

The forty-seven miles of low-traffic greenery is due to a profusion of county parks. Totaling over 14,000 acres, this plethora of grass, trees, and open space takes the form of both established parks with stone shelters, like Brown Deer Park, and scenic parkways—winding, serpentine corridors through urban and suburban areas—like the Oak Creek Parkway near the start of your ride.

There are a few problems with the trail, which is why we include such detailed directions. Some of the signs are missing; others are turned around. There are so many bike paths in some places that it's easy to take a wrong turn and become lost. And a map that the parks commission provides shows only some of the road names and the roads themselves, so beware.

The ride has some diverse attractions. You'll ride past the

Milwaukee Art Center, along the lakefront, near the busy McKinley Marina, with slips for 350 boats, and the Milwaukee Yacht Club, with its nautical vessels of all sizes and shapes berthed nearby. You'll see the homes of the rich and the used-to-be-rich, and you can inspect an Italianate mansion at close range if you go into the Villa Terrace Decorative Arts Museum on North Terrace Avenue.

The ride even passes through part of downtown where, if you look closely at some of the shop names, you might see a trace of the German influence that everyone associates with the city. (At one time, two out of every three Milwaukeeans who bought a paper bought one in German.) This heritage may be part of the reason Milwaukee not only manufactures beer but also boasts that it consumes more beer than anywhere else in the country. Even the concessions at the lakefront parks at the north end of the city sell beer along with hot dogs and Coca-Cola. (Be careful on your spin through these parks. On summer weekends they are jammed with roller skaters with widely varying degrees of balance. Use the park road if you have to.)

This ride makes a good weekend trip if you spend the night somewhere in the city. But if you complete the loop in a day, don't zip right out of the city. If you've never explored this amalgam, you're missing an experience.

Time your ride to include one of the many Lake Michigan festivals, such as the Lakefront Festival of the Arts in Juneau Park in July (which is along the ride); Summerfest, with its international folk festival, bazaar, and circus, south of downtown; and, in the same spot, the Fiesta Italiana, with entertainment, a midway, and a traditional Italian procession.

Or just stay around to sample the food. Milwaukee has Greek, French, Chinese, and, of course, lots of German and Polish (the city's second-largest ethnic group) restaurants. After all, seventy-six miles of biking can work up quite an appetite.

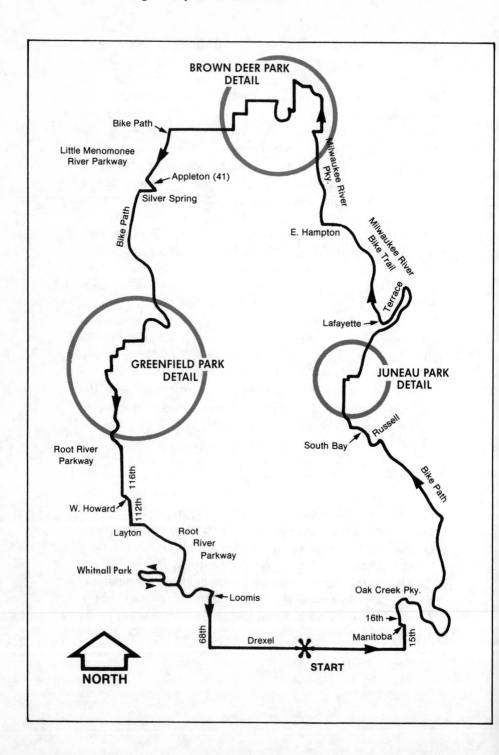

BROWN DEER PARK
DETAIL

Bike Path

Little Menomonee
River Parkway

Appleton (41)

Silver Spring

Bike Path

Milwaukee River
Pky.

E. Hampton

Milwaukee River
Bike Trail

Terrace

Lafayette

GREENFIELD PARK
DETAIL

JUNEAU PARK
DETAIL

Russell

Root River
Parkway

South Bay

116th

Bike Path

W. Howard

112th

Layton

Root
River
Parkway

Whitnall Park

Oak Creek Pky.

Loomis

16th

Manitoba

15th

68th

Drexel

START

NORTH

Seventy-Sixer

Begin anywhere near where Drexel Avenue crosses over
I-94. The road has frequently heavy traffic and narrow shoulders. Go

(L) north on 15th Street

(L) west on Manitoba

(R) north on 16th, across the bridge, where it becomes Oak
    Creek Parkway. Follow the parkway as it curves. A
    separate path runs next to the road at times. A separate
    bike path begins soon after you enter Grant Park. You
    follow it about 7 miles through several parks. At the
    north end of South Shore Park, just after the yacht club,
    turn

(L) west on East Russell

(R) north on South Bay

(R) north on 1st Street, over a drawbridge, past some an-
    cient factories. 1st Street merges with Kinnikinnic,
    passes the Allen Bradley clock and neighborhood work-
    ers' bars. Then turn

(R) east on Pittsburgh

(L) north on South Water

(R) north on North Water

(R) east on St. Paul

(L) north on Van Buren

(R) east on Clybourn

(L) north on Harbor (also called Lincoln Memorial Drive),
    past Milwaukee Art Center. Turn at the Art Center to
    get on Juneau Park bike paths. Follow Lincoln Memorial
    Drive to a University of Wisconsin–Milwaukee sign.
    Turn

(L) west on bike path through the park, which curves south
    and becomes Terrace Drive

(R) west on Lafayette; watch for a road that branches left
    down a hill, just before Lafayette crosses an overpass.
    Between the road and the overpass is a sidewalk; follow

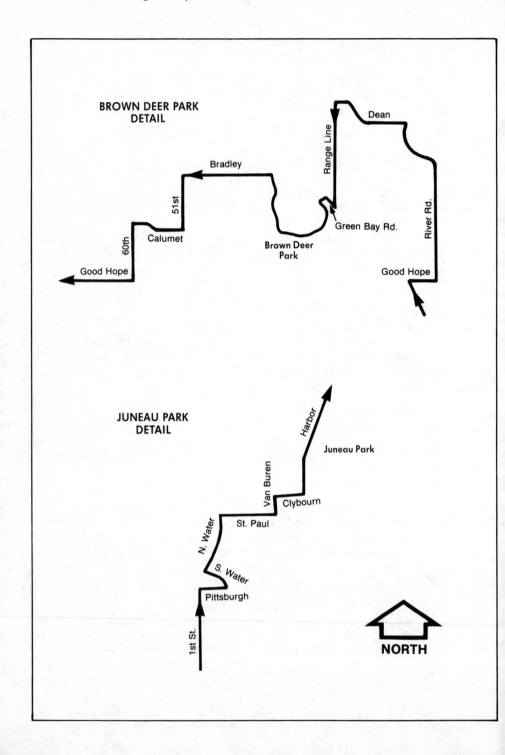

it left, downhill, to the beginning of the Milwaukee River Bike Trail (sometimes follows parkway road, sometimes a separate bike path). Then

(L) west on East Hampton

(R) north on Milwaukee River Parkway

(R) east on Good Hope Road

(L) north on North River Road

(L) west on Dean (don't turn right on another Dean that crops up)

(L) south on Range Line Road, over the Milwaukee River

(R) north on Green Bay Road, jog

(L) west, then another left into Brown Deer Park. Turn left when you see turnoff for Bradley Road, then

(L) west on Bradley

(L) south on North 51st, past Algonquin Park

(R) west on Calumet at the Golf Club

(L) south on North 60th

(R) west on Good Hope, past Noyes Park. Turn left at sign, onto bike path, at North 91st. The path stops at Leon Road; go straight, on Little Menomonee River Parkway, to

(L) southeast on Appleton (U.S. 41)

(R) west on Silver Spring, past Loehmann's, and across the river. Watch for beginning of bike path on the left side. The path forks just before Wisconsin 100. Take a sharp right to an underpass under the highway; you'll merge again with the parkway later on. Then

(R) south on Swan, under railroad tracks

(R) west on Underwood, which curves around to

(R) west on Watertown Plank Road and across river and tracks

(L) south on 115th

(R) west on Underwood

(L) south on 119th

(R) west on Potter

(L) south on 121st and across Blue Mound Road

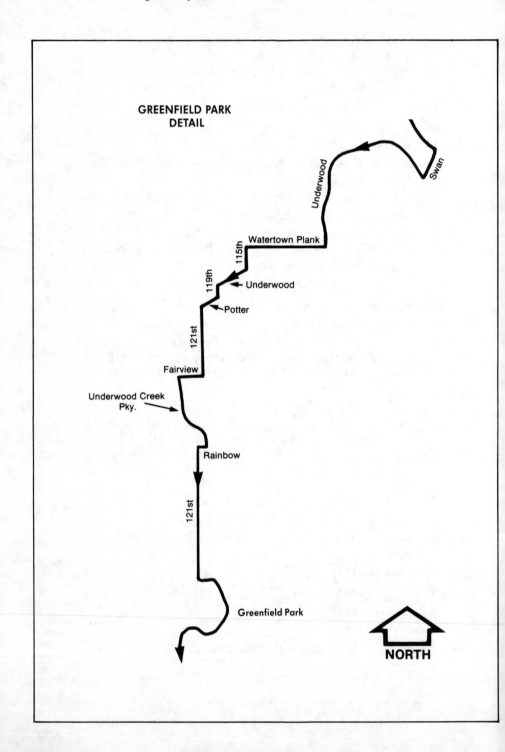

**GREENFIELD PARK
DETAIL**

Swan

Underwood

Watertown Plank

115th

119th

Underwood

Potter

121st

Fairview

Underwood Creek
Pky.

Rainbow

121st

Greenfield Park

NORTH

(R) west on Fairview. Fairview turns left and becomes

(L) south, Underwood Creek Parkway, which turns into two roads. Take the one to the right, then

(R) west on Rainbow Avenue

(L) south on 121st, across Greenfield and into Greenfield Golf Course. Root River Bike Trail begins. Turn left at first park road, then right at the T, and right at the next fork, out of the park, across Lincoln, and onto the Root River Parkway. Turn south on 116th, then

(L) east on West Howard

(R) south on 112th, across Beloit

(L) east on Layton

(R) south on Root River Parkway. Continue on Root River Parkway across South 76th Street.

Or **detour**

(R) north on 92nd, then follow Whitnall Park Drive to see the Botanical Gardens. Retrace path to Root River Parkway and follow it to

(R) south on Loomis, at the large white Kinette Building

(L) south on 68th Street, across Rawson

(L) east on Drexel to Start.

Sugar River Trail
New Glarus

Location:	Southern Wisconsin, about 120 miles from Chicago
Distance:	46 miles round trip
Traffic:	None
Camping:	New Glarus Woods State Park
Difficulty:	Easy, but this is a fairly long round-trip ride
Riding time:	7–9 hours
Directions:	Take Interstate 90 to Beloit, Wisconsin, then go west on Wisconsin 81 and north on Wisconsin 11 to Brodhead. Or you can continue to the intersection with Wisconsin 69 and turn north on 69 to New Glarus.

It has been many years since the trains of the Chicago, Milwaukee, St. Paul and Pacific moved through the Sugar River country, past the hayfields, Holsteins, and stately silos of this tranquil but intensely productive dairying region.

213

But thousands of people still enjoy the lush greenery along the railroad's right-of-way each year. The tracks are gone; in their place is a state-operated, twenty-three-mile-long biking and hiking trail connecting the hamlets of Brodhead and New Glarus.

The Sugar River Trail is slightly beyond the range of this book, but it's so popular with Illinoisans and such a worthwhile trip that we decided to include it. A better introduction to medium-length bike trips, and to southern Wisconsin, would be hard to find.

The caretaker at the old depot that serves as trail headquarters says more than 35,000 people ride here each year, though they are comfortably dispersed over time and the length of the trail, so it rarely seems crowded. He has seen eighty-five-year-olds complete the ride, as well as a two-week-old infant, asleep in mama's backpack within the first mile.

There are bikes for rent in each of the four communities along the trail, and in each, arrangements can be made for car service to pick up wearied riders.

Most riders begin the trail at New Glarus, perhaps because, in contrast to the other towns along the route, it is an occasionally bustling tourist attraction.

Advertised as "Heidiland, U.S.A." and "Little Switzerland," New Glarus has some of the blandishments you'll find in any tourist-oriented town—the ethnic holidays, food, and architecture that mix tradition with salability. But New Glarus is mostly free of fakery and inflated prices. Even on the loveliest late spring day, there were no throngs of people, no traffic jams on the little Main Street.

New Glarus was settled in 1845 by a group of 108 Swiss from the canton of Glarus, emigrants to a vast, empty new land from their narrow and overpopulated mountain valley (Switzerland is only a fifth as large as Wisconsin). Most had been textile workers who lost their jobs to the mechanized looms of the inexorable Industrial Revolution. The first years in their new home were hard. One of the first settlers wrote that the women seemed always to be weeping, partly from homesickness, partly from exhaustion.

Visitors may still hear the Swiss-German dialect on the streets of New Glarus, and there is a strong hint of Alpine Europe in the faces and the accents. The phone book is full of the names of founding families: Hoesli, Luchsinger, Stuessy, Klassy, Kubly, Tschudy.

Ties with the homeland are exceptionally strong. Swiss tourists visit each week in spring and summer. The Swiss government sends exhibits for the pioneer museum. Grade-schoolers cultivate pen pals in old Glarus. And more than a few in New Glarus have visited their ancestral home. One group among the citizenry plays the traditional Alphorn, that ten-foot-long instrument that resembles an uncoiled cornucopia and sounds like an elephant with a beautifully clear vibrato. Modernists may wear Swiss Power T-shirts.

At the Swiss Historical Village just north of town, several log cabins house early-day dairy equipment, farm implements, a one-room schoolhouse, and one small building of which the Swiss-Americans are very proud—a cabin built during the settlement's second summer. It was recently discovered, camouflaged under the walls of an old farmhouse about to be razed. It had been used as a washroom after the "new" building was constructed over and around it. Now, carefully disassembled beam by beam and re-erected at the Historical Village, it stands in the most prominent corner.

Swiss people still immigrate to the area today. Teresa and Ernest Jaggi, who work at the Town Hall Dairy a few miles from New Glarus, arrived from Bern about twenty years ago. Theirs is one of eighty cheese factories in Green County, which manufactures more Swiss cheese than any other in the country. We watched the Jaggis laugh together as they deftly moved the enormous blocks and wheels of pungent cheese from place to place in the factory. They reduce 45,000 pounds of milk to twenty-three 180-pound cheeses each day.

The trail passes through prairie grasslands that are still as the settlers found them—untouched by the plow. It frequently bridges small streams over the foundations of the old railroad trestles. In the quiet of early morning we surprised chipmunks, squirrels, cottontails, plenty of cows, cardinals, red-winged blackbirds, and two lumbering, grumpy turtles.

Each of the little communities along the trail has its own character, though their ethnicity is less apparent than New Glarus's.

Monticello, population 870. Dead center in the single block of "downtown" is an obliging drugstore with drinks for a hot day. Over the years the pharmacist, his yellow smock buttoned up to the neck, has inadvertently created on his shelves a museum of outdated advertising displays celebrating the virtues of cold remedies, laxatives, film, and dairy products. The life-sized cardboard Kodak swimsuit girls of 1959 and 1979 smile winningly at each other across the room, identical except for their hairstyles and apparel.

A few miles farther on is Albany, population 875. The trail skirts its western edge, but the ride into town climbs a substantial hill. Linden's Corner is a small variety store there with a felt-penned sign in its window: Bikers Welcome. We bought ice-cream cones for an improbable thirty-five cents for 2½ scoops, forty-five cents for 3½. Even with the smaller size, we had to lick fast to keep up.

Albany is at the sparkling confluence of the Little and Big Sugar rivers. Small children, and sometimes their parents, scale a chain-link fence to fish from the concrete foundations of a century-old powerhouse at the river's edge. As we watched, a boy pulled out a four-pound carp with modesty, though his young friends seemed suitably impressed. There is canoeing, water-skiing, and three parks nearby, but this is hardly a tourist mecca. Cars pass through only once in a while, especially on weekday afternoons. For those of us who can adapt to the rhythms of such restful places, a long nap in the grass under some bur oaks is close at hand.

The southern terminus of the trail is Brodhead, a supply center for farmers. We returned to New Glarus by car to take home a fat wedge of fresh cheese, many cookies, fresh rye bread, and some summer sausage. As railroads go, this one is a success worth celebrating. Amtrak should be so good.

More Rides and Routes

More rides and routes you can send away for:

Cycle Chicago
Mayor's Office of Inquiry and Information
City Hall
Chicago, IL 60602

Boone County Conservation District
522½ South State Street
Belvidere, IL 61008

DeKalb County Forest Preserve District
104 North Main
Sycamore, IL 60178

The Prairie Path
P.O. Box 1086
Wheaton, IL 60187

Forest Preserve District of Cook County
536 North Harlem Avenue
River Forest, IL 60305

Illinois Department of Tourism
222 South College Street
Springfield, IL 62706

The Palatine Trail
262 East Palatine Road
Palatine, IL 60067

Three Oaks Spokes Bicycle Club
303 East Michigan Street
Three Oaks, MI 49128

Bicentennial Bike Map of Wisconsin
Wisconsin Division of Tourism
Department of Business Development
P.O. Box 7606
Madison, WI 53707